602

4629187941

2F-1

The Study of Names in Literature: A Bibliography

Elizabeth M. Rajec

Assistant Professor
Cohen Library, CCNY

K.G. SAUR PUBLISHING INC.

K.G. SAUR PUBLISHING INC.
175 Fifth Avenue
New York, NY   10010
Tel. (212)477-2500
Telex 238386 KGSP UR

Library of Congress Cataloging in Publication Data

Rajec, Elizabeth M
    The study of names in literature.

    Includes index.
    1. Names, Personal, in literature--Indexes.
2. Names, Personal--Indexes.   I.   Title.
Z6514.N35R34 [PN56.4]   016.809'92   78-2095
ISBN 0-89664-000-0

Printed and bound in the United States of America,
by Edwards Brothers, Inc.

"Nomen et omen."

"Nomen est omen."

VITA

Elizabeth M. Rajec is Chief of Acquisitions at the
Cohen Library, City College of the City University
of New York. She received her B.S. from Columbia
University, her M.L.S. from Rutgers, the State University, and her Ph.D. from the City University of
New York. She has in print a bibliography on German
literary onomastics, has compiled a bibliography on
reclassification, and has also published on names
and their meanings in Franz Kafka's works.

CONTENTS

FOREWORD

The present bibliography is an outgrowth of the author's "Literarische Onomastik: Eine Bibliographie," published as Beihefte der <u>Beiträge zur Namenforschung</u> (Heidelberg: Carl Winter, 1977) and is designed as a strong first step toward the eventual production of a comprehensive bibliography in literary onomastics. The need for such a bibliography is great: no such catalogue exists at present, and those who would know how a particular author chose his names or, on the other hand, how a particular name has been used by various authors must search through a formidable array of separate compilations and their supplements.

As we have indicated, this bibliography, although extensive, does not pretend to be complete. As librarian at a major American university, however, the author is in a position to know about an exceptionally wide range of works in literary onomastics, in itself an assurance of competency and accuracy.

Dr. Rajec's bibliography should therefore provide the scholar with a handy and reliable aid in his investigation of literary names, and we welcome its inclusion among the source materials of onomatology.

C. M. Rothrauff

PREFACE

Ever since Aristotle pointed out that names in literature are creative elements, many authors have been fascinated by them and have coined names for their characters with great care; but only lately has onomastics as a consciously employed device become part of literary criticism in general. Perhaps the fact that scholarly studies of names are a fairly recent development explains conjointly that no bibliography on names in literature has yet appeared. Thus, the "raison d'être" of this bibliography is as a primer - to provide for the first time a survey of the most important studies in literary onomastics.

PURPOSE

The Study of Names in Literature: A Bibliography is designed to offer a dual service to its user. First, its purpose is to assist the scholar, the librarian, and the researcher interested in the specific topic of literary onomastics in locating name studies. Second, it supplements the studies on names in literature with carefully selected reference sources that deal with onomastics in general. Basically, the design of this guide is broadly based; it is not exhaustive, neither is it selective in any strict sence. Nevertheless,

its purpose is to fill the gap of a needed reference
tool by consolidating the specific as well as the
general references on onomastics in a single mono-
graph.

<u>SCOPE</u>

The material included in the bibliography offers a
selection of:

1. Primary entries
   (authors' comments on their coinage and
   usage of names)

2. Secondary entries
   (interpretations of onomastics, ranging from
   dissertations and scholarly works to short
   articles)

3. Reviews of studies on names in literature

4. A spectrum of reference sources
   (ranging from general name dictionaries by
   languages or topics to theoretical onomastics)

Because of the voluminous scope of available name sources
this bibliography does not attempt to be all-inclusive.
It is - just as names are by their very nature - international in scope. Therefore, selected foreign language
publications, important to the serious researcher are
included, despite the risk that they might not be easily
available. In addition, we have included a number of
references published as late as the end of 1977. As a
carefully compiled bibliography it hopes to satisfy with
its selections - ranging from unique titles to sources

most frequently in demand - even the most resourceful and demanding person. In general, only entries were included that deal with specific authors' usage of names (including the origin, history, and etymology of any given name). As in any selection, here too, a subjective coloring was unavoidable. Ultimately, only the user can determine the extent to which it meets his or her needs.

ARRANGEMENT

The book is composed of two parts: an Author Index and a Subject Index. In the Author Index, bibliographic entries are arranged by author in a single alphabetical sequence. Several entries by the same author are placed within their alphabetical sequence by title. Even at the risk of redundancy, cross references have been added for multiple authors, editors, and the like, whenever the slightest need for such an aid seemed advisable. Each bibliographic citation is preceded by a number which also appears in the Subject Index. Thus, the number cited in the alphabetically arranged Subject Index does not refer to pages but to the number affixed to each entry. Cross indexing of subjects is also provided for. Where subjects overlap, they are double- or multiple-listed in the index. Whenever possible, sources are cited in full rather than abbreviated. Journal title, volume, date, and paging -

all are given; in the case of monographs, author, title, place, publisher, date, and - if applicable - series are included. In general, alphabetizing follows the practice of the Library of Congress; de, la, von, etc., whenever necessary, are cross indexed.

The annotation notes are brief in character. Their primary purpose is to indicate the subject matter when the title does not reveal it, or when the title is in a foreign language. The notes never intend to evaluate.

SOURCES AND ACKNOWLEDGEMENTS

As previously stated, the purpose of this bibliography is to create a panoramic view of available studies of names in literature. A task of this nature cannot be accomplished without consolidating information available from many sources. Therefore, I am most indebted to all those known and unknown persons who edited, compiled, and labored in the field of onomastics in the past. I am particularly indebted to Elsdon C. Smith's Personal Names: A Bibliography and to the yearly supplements in Names, which include entries on literary onomastics and are listed here. Some of the German entries were supplied by Rudolf Schützeichel, editor of Beiträge zur Namenforschung, and a few of the other non-English entries are taken from Bibliographical Onomastica and Onoma, edited by Willy van Langendonck. In addition,

many fine articles cited in this bibliography owe their
publication to the efforts of Grace Alvarez-Altman,
editor of Literary Onomastics Studies, a publication
devoted exclusively to names in literature, and to Fred
Tarpley, Editor of the Publications of the South Central
Names Institute. And finally, I would like to express
my appreciation to Conrad M. Rothrauff, editor of Names,
for his kindness in writing the Foreword to this bibliography.

Also serving as sources for studies in literary onomastics
were the National Union Catalog of the Library of Congress,
The Dictionary Catalog of the Research Libraries of the
New York Public Library, Dissertation Abstracts International, Humanities Index, and Reader's Guide to Periodical
Literature, just to mention a few. Whenever possible,
items were requested through interlibrary loan and
examined for accuracy.

The following periodicals include material on onomastics
and, with the exception of a few volumes, were consulted:

Anthroponymica. Instituut voor Naamkunde.
    Leuven.
        Vol. 1-   (1947-   )

Beiträge zur Namenforschung.
　　Heidelberg.
　　　　Vol. 1-16 (1949/50-65)

　　　　Neue Folge, vol. 1-　　　(1966-　　)

　　　　Beihefte.
　　　　　　No. 1-　　　(1969-　　)

Literary Onomastics Studies.
　　Brockport, N.Y.
　　　　Vol. 1-　　　(1974-　　)

Mitteilungen für Namenkunde. Arbeitskreis für
　　Namenforschung.
　　Aachen.
　　　　(Irregular)
　　　　Supersedes Nachrichtenblatt für (deutsche)
　　　　Flurnamenkunde.

Naamkunde. Mededelingen von het Instituut voor Naamkunde
　　te Leuven en de Commissie voor Naamkunde en
　　Nederzettingsgeschiedenis.
　　Amsterdam.

Namenkundliche Informationen.
　　Continued by the Informationen der Leipziger
　　namenkundlichen Arbeitergruppe an der Karl-Marx-
　　Universität.
　　Leipzig.

Names. Journal of the American Name Society.
　　Berkeley.
　　　　Vol. 1-　　　(1953-　　)

Onoma. Bulletin d'Information et de Bibliographie.
　　Bibliographical and Information Bulletin.
　　International Centre of Onomastics.
　　International Committee of Onomastic Sciences.
　　Louvain.
　　　　Vol. 1-　　　(1950-　　)

Onomastica. Pismo poswiecone nazewnictwu giograficznemu
i osobowemu.
Wroclaw.
Vol. 1-   (1955-   )

Onomastica. Revue Internationale de Toponymie et
d'Anthroponymie.
Paris.
Vol. 1-2.   (1947-1948)
Continued by Revue Internationale d'Ono-
mastique.

Onomastica. Ukrainian Free Academy of Sciences.
Canadian Institute of Onomastic Sciences.
Winnipeg.
Vol. 1-   (1951-   )

Onomastica Jugoslavica. Meduakademijski Odbor za
Onomastiku.
Ljubljana.
Vol. 1-   (1969-   )

Onomastica Slavogermanica. Sächsische Akademie der
Wissenschaften. Philologische-historische Klasse.
Abhandlungen. (Issued alternately by the Univer-
sity of Breslau.)
Leipzig.
Vol. 1-   (1965-   )

Onomasticon. Tutto sul tuo nome.
Milan.
Vol. 1-   (1964-   )

Onomata. Revue d'Onomastique Grecque.
Athens.
Vol. 1-   (1952-   )

Publications of the South Central Names Institute.
East Texas State University.
Commerce, Texas.
Vol. 1-   (1972-   )

Revue Internationale d'Onomastique.
    Paris.
            Vol. 1-   (1949-   )
            Supersedes Onomastica.

The author would be most appreciative of any suggestions
or corrections but particularly of additions that any
user may care to provide. They may write to me c/o
City College of the City University of New York, Cohen
Library, 135th Street at Convent Avenue, New York,
New York, 10031. I should make clear that the gaps
and possible errors or shortcomings are entirely my
own responsibility. A last word, one of sincere
apology, is due to those whose names were inadvertently
overlooked.

                                    Elizabeth M. Rajec

AUTHOR INDEX

1   Abel, Otto
         Die deutschen Personen-Namen. Berlin, Hertz,
         1899.

         See also later editions by Walter Robert-Tornow.
         On German personal names.

2   Abramowitz, Barbara Hillson
         Don Quijote's Ambiguous Names.   Johns Hopkins
         University, 1970.

         A dissertation on Cervantes's names.

3   Abrams, Fred
         "Cervantes' Berganza-Cipión Anagrams in 'El
         coloquio de los perros'," Names, 24 (1976)
         325-6.

4   ---, "Onomastic Humor in Saki's Filboid Studge, the
         Story of the Mouse That Helped," Names, 19
         (1971), 287-8.

         On names by Munro.

5   Ackerman, Robert William
         An Index of the Arthurian Names in Middle
         English.   Stanford, Stanford University Press,
         1952.   (Stanford University Publication Series,
         Language and Literature, Vol. 10)

6   Adams, Joseph Quincy
         A Life of William Shakespeare.   Boston, Houghton,
         1923.

         See pp. 1-8 on Shakespeare's name.

7   Adolf, H.
         "A Review of G. Schramm's 'Namenschatz ...',"
         Journal of English and Germanic Philology, 57
         (1958), 89-90.

         On Germanic personal names.

---, See: 1042.

8   Aebischer, Paul
    "A Review of P. R. Menéndez' 'La Chanson de
    Roland'," Zeitschrift für romanische Philo-
    logie, 76 (1960), 259-65.

    On names in the "Chanson de Roland."

---, See: 764.

9   Ageeva, R. A.
    "Toponimika v trudach M. A. Kastrena,"
    Razvitie metodov toponimičeskich issledovanij.
    Moskva, 1970.

    On toponyma in the works of Castrén, see pp.
    73-80.

    Ahally, S.
    See: 807.

    Ahvledinai, G. S.
    See: 233.

10 Albertos Firmat, María Lourdes
    La onomastica personal primitiva de Hispania
    Terraconense y Bética. Salamanca, Nebrija,
    1966. (Theses et studia philologica Sala-
    manticensia, 13)

    On Spanish personal names.

11 Alderman, Taylor
    "The Begetting of Gatsby," Modern Fiction
    Studies, 19 (Winter 1973-4), 563-5.

    On names by F. Scott Fitzgerald.

12 Alerič, Daniel
    "Oronimi Kunara: Jadika," Onomastica Jugo-
    slavica (Zagreb), 3 (1973-4), 3-21.

    On names in Croatian folksongs.

13   Alfonsin, Edward J.
        "A Review of E. C. Smith's 'Personal Names:
        A Bibliography'," Names, 14 (1966), 127.

       ---, See: 1111.

14   Algeo, John
        On Defining the Proper Name. Gainesville, Uni-
        versity of Florida Press, 1973. (University of
        Florida Humanities Monograph No. 41)

       ---, See: 339.

15   Allen, Charles
        Notes on the Bacon-Shakespeare Question.
        Boston, Houghton, 1900.

        See pp. 14-6 on the spelling of Shakespeare's
        name.

16   Allen, D. C.
        "Milton and the Name of Eve," Modern Language
        Notes, 74 (1959), 681-3.

17   Alter, J.
        "Le jeu des noms dans Polexandre," Romanic
        Review, 67 (1976), 9-27.

        On punning with names in the Polexandre.

      Altheim, Franz
        See: 758.

      Altman, Grace Alvarez
        See: Alvarez-Altman, Grace

18   Alvarez-Altman, Grace
        "Onomastics as a Modern Critical Approach to
        Literature," Literary Onomastics Studies, 1
        (1974), 103-11.

        On literary onomastics.

19   Amirov, G. S.
      "Onomastik v proizvedenijach Gabduly Tukaja"
      in Onomastika Povolž'ja. Mater, Ul'janovsk,
      1969.

      On names in the works of Abdulah Tuka, see
      pp. 68-74.

20   Anagnostopoulus, Georgios
      "Plato's Cratylus: The Two Theories of the
      Correctness of Names," The Review of Metaphysics,
      25 (1972), 691-736.

21   Andreeva, L. I.
      "Antroponimija v trilogii A. N. Ostrovskogo o
      Bal'zaminove," Onomastika Povolž'ja, 2 (1971),
      311-5.

      On personal names in the trilogy of A. N.
      Ostrovskij.

22   Andresen, Karl Gustav
      Die altdeutschen Personennamen in ihrer Entwick-
      lung und Erscheinung als heutige Geschlechtsnamen.
      Mainz, Kunze, 1876. Reprint: Walluf, Sändig,
      1977.

      On Old Germanic personal names.

23   Apperson, George Latimer
      "Some Shakespearean Names," The Gentleman's
      Magazine, 287 (September 1899), 278-83.

24   Aristotle
      Peri poietike. (On the Art of Poetry). Kom-
      mentar von Alfred Gudeman. Berlin, de Gruyter,
      1934.

      On literary onomastics, see pp. 42, and 200-10.
      See also other editions.

25 Arndt, Wilhelm
        Die Personennamen der deutschen Schauspiele des
        Mittelalters. Breslau, Marcus, 1904. (Germa-
        nistische Abhandlungen, Heft 23)

        On personal names in German medieval dramas.

26 Arnold, Robert Franz
        Die deutschen Vornamen. Ein Vortrag. Wien,
        Holzhausen, 1900.

        On German first names. See also 2nd edition,
        1901.

27 Arthur, William
        An Etymological Dictionary of Family and Chris-
        tian Names; With an Essay on Their Derivation
        and Import. New York, Sheldon, 1857. Reprint:
        Detroit, Gale, 1969.

28 Ashley, Leonard R. N.
        "Flicks, Flacks, and Flux: Tides of Taste in
        the Onomasticon of the Moving Picture Industry,"
        Names, 23 (1975), 221-80.

        Refers also to literary works.

29 Ashton, Thomas L.
        "Naming Byron's Aurora Raby," English Language
        Notes, 7 (1969), 114-20.

30 Astour, Michael C.
        "Semitic Elements in the Kumarbi Myth: An
        Onomastic Inquiry," Journal of Near Eastern
        Studies, 27 (1968), 172-7.

        On names in the Kumarbi epic.

31 Athanassakis, A.
        "An Inquiry Into the Etymology and Meaning of
        Iphthimos in the Early Epic," Glotta, 49
        (1971), 1-21.

32   Auer, M. J.
         "Caddy, Benjy, and the 'Acts of the Apostles':
         A Note on 'The Sound and the Fury'," <u>Studies
         in the Novel</u>, 6 (1974), 475-6.

         On the names in above work by Faulkner.

33   <u>Aus dem Namengut Mitteleuropas</u>. Kulturberührung im
         deutsch-romanisch-slawobaltischen Sprachraum.
         Festgabe zum 75. Geburtstag von Eberhard
         Kranzmayer. Hrsg. von Maria und Herwig Hans
         Hornung. Klagenfurt, Landesmuseum, 1972.
         (Kärtner Museumschriften, Nr. 53)

         A collection of essays on Middle European
         names.

34   Austin, James Curtiss
         <u>The Significant Name in Terence</u>. University
         of Illinois at Urbana Champaign, 1921.

         A dissertation.

35   Avni, Abraham A.
         "Hugo's Alleged Fabrications of Names and Anach-
         ronisms," <u>Modern Language Notes</u>, 79 (1964),
         264-9.

         On names in the works of Victor Hugo.

36   Axtell, Harold Lucius
         "Men's Names in the Writings of Cicero,"
         <u>Classical Philology</u>, 10 (1915), 386-404.

37   Axton, William
         "Esther's Nicknames: A Study in Relevance,
         "<u>The Dickensian</u>, 62 (1966), 158-63.

         On Names in "Bleak House" by Dickens.

38   Ayer, Alfred James
         <u>The Concept of a Person and Other Essays</u>.
         New York, St. Martin's, 1963.

         See pp. 129-61 on "Names and Descriptions."

39   Bach, Adolf
      Deutsche Namenkunde. 3 vols in 5. Heidelberg,
      Winter, 1952-6.

      Index by Dieter Berger. On German literary
      onomastics, see I, 277; I, 293; I, 505; and
      I, 529. See also 2nd edition, 1974.

      ---, See: 132, 306, 761, 823, 1053.

40   Bachmann, Ingeborg
      Gedichte, Erzählungen, Hörspiel, Essays. Piper
      München, 1964. (Die Bücher der Neunzehn, Bd.
      111)

      See pp. 313-29 on names by Kafka, Th. Mann,
      Joyce, and Proust.

      Bachofer, Wolfgang
      See: 637.

41   Backus, Joseph M.
      "Gelett Burgess and Names for Characters,"
      Names, 9 (1961), 95-107.

42   ---, "I Never Done a Burgess! Three Unpublished
      Letters from 'Booth Tarkington' Touched Off
      by His Use of a Name," Names, 12 (1964),
      137-53.

43   ---, "Names of Characters in Faulkner's 'The Sound
      and the Fury'," Names, 6 (1958), 226-33.

44   ---, "'Poor Valentin' or 'Monsieur le Comte': Vari-
      ation in Character Designation as Matter for
      Critical Consideration (in Henry James' 'The
      American')," Names, 20 (1972), 47-55.

45   ---, "Two 'No-Name' Poems," Names, 15 (1967), 1-7.

      On poems by E. Dickinson and e. e. cummings.

---, See: 1156.

46 Baehr, R.
        "A Review of Morley-Tyler's 'Los nombres ...',"
        Die neueren Sprachen, N. F. 11 (1962), 246-7.

        On names by Lope de Vega.

    ---, See: 802.

47 Baesecke, Georg
        "Gudrun-Kriemhilt, Grimhild-Uote, Guthorm-
        Gernot," Beiträge zur Geschichte der deutschen
        Sprache und Literatur, 60 (1936), 371-80.

        On names in Germanic heroic literature.

48 Bahlow, Hans
        Alteuropas Namenwelt und ihre Erforschung.
        Eine Denkschrift. Hamburg, Bahlow, 1958.

        On the history of old Europe's names.

49 ---, Deutsches Namenbuch. Ein Führer durch
        Deutschlands Familiennamen. Neumünster,
        Wachholtz, 1933.

        On the etymology of German family names.

50 ---, Deutsches Namenlexikon. Familien- und Vornamen
        nach Ursprung und Sinn erklärt. Müchen, Keyser,
        1967. Reprint: Suhrkamp, 1972.

        A lexicon of German family and first names. See
        particularly p. 7 on literary onomastics.

51 ---, Namenforschung als Wissenschaft. Deutschlands
        Ortsnamen als Denkmäler keltischer Vorzeit.
        Neumünster, Wachholtz, 1955.

        Onomastics as science. Mainly on German-
        Celtic geographical names.

52   ---, Unsere Vornamen im Wandel der Jahrhunderte.
         Limburg, Starke, 1965. (Grundriss der
         Genealogie, Bd. 4)

         On German first names.

53   Bahner, W.
         "A Review of Morley-Tyler's 'Los nombres ...',"
         Deutsche Literaturzeitung, 83 (1962), 636-7.

         On names by Lope de Vega.

         ---, See: 802.

54   Bühnisch, Alfred
         Die deutschen Personennamen. Leipzig, Teubner,
         1910. (Aus Natur und Geisteswelt: Sammlung
         wissenschaftlichgemeinverständlicher Darstel-
         lungen, Bd. 296)

         On German personal names. See also later
         edition, 1920. See particularly p. 108.

55   Baker, Christopher P.
         "Salerio, Solanio, Salarino, and Salario,"
         Names, 23 (1975), 56-7.

         On the above names by Shakespeare.

56   Baker, R. L., and R. C. Frushell
         "Defoe's Blow-Bladder Street in 'A Journal
         of the Plague Year'," Journal of American
         Folklore, 87 (1974), 160-2.

         On names by Defoe.

57   Baldensperger, F.
         "Notes sur deux noms propres de la Comédie
         humaine," Modern Language Notes, 60 (1945),
         50-2.

         On names by Balzac.

         Ball, Patricia M.
         See: 608.

58   Barber, Henry
           British Family Names. Their Origin and Meaning.
           With lists of Scandinavian, Frisian, Anglo-Saxon,
           and Norman Names. London, Stock, 1894.

           On English family names. See also 2nd edition,
           1903.

59   "The Bard of Avon's Name," Miscellaneous Notes and
           Queries (American), 1 (February 1884), 305-7.

           On Shakespeare.

60   Bardsley, Charles Wareing Endell
           Curiosities of Puritan Nomenclature. London,
           Windus, 1880.

           On English personal names. See also the
           edition of 1897.

61   ---, A Dictionary of English and Welsh Surnames with
           Special American Instances. London, Frowde, 1901.

           See later edition, 1904. See also reprint, 1967.

62   ---, English Surnames: Their Sources and Signifi-
           cations. London, Chatto, 1875.

           See also reprint with new introduction by
           L. G. Pine, Newton Abbot, David, 1969.

63   Barker, Howard Frederick
           "The Family Names of American Negros,"
           American Speech, 14 (1939), 163-74.

64   ---, "How We Got Our Surnames," American Speech,
           4 (October 1928), 48-53.

65   ---, "Our Leading Surnames," American Speech,
           1 (1926), 470-7.

66   ---, "Queer Names," American Speech, 6 (December
           1930), 101-9.

67   -—, "Surnames," <u>American Speech</u>, 2 (April 1927), 332-3.

68   ---, "Surnames in the United States," <u>The American Mercury</u>, 26 (1932), 223-30.

69   Barnes, John L.
"Lady Bellaston: Fielding's Use of the Charactonym," in <u>Of Edsels and Marauders</u>. Ed. by F. Tarpley and A. Moseley. Commerce, Texas, Names Institute Press, 1971. (South Central Names Institute Publication No. 1)

See pp. 114-6.

70   Barnett, M. J.
"Porpaillart in the Cycle de Guillaume d'Orange," <u>The Modern Language Review</u>, 66 (1971), 772-4.

On the above toponym.

71   Barnhart, Clarence Lewis
"Index (to Vols. 1-15)," <u>Names</u>, 15 (1967), 245-340.

On literary names, see pp. 287, and 296-7.

72   ---, <u>New Century Cyclopedia of Names</u>.

---, See: 838.

73   Barrère, Jean Bertrand
"Hugo jaugé par Balzac; ou, L'étrange cas onomastique de 'La cousine Bette'," <u>Mercure de France</u>, 308 (1950), 103-14.

On names by Hugo and Balzac.

74   Barrus, Paul W.
      "Literary Names in American Literature," in
      Of Edsels and Marauders. Ed. by F. Tarpley
      and A. Moseley. Commerce, Texas, Names
      Institute Press, 1971. (South Central Names
      Institute Publication No. 1)

      See pp. 73-4.

75   Barth, E.
      "Zur Theorie der Struktur des Namens,"
      Naamkunde, 1 (1969), 41-4.

      On the theory of name structure.

76   Barthold, Eberhard
      Seifensieder Unschlitt und Madame Chauchat.
      Die Eigennamen in Thomas Manns Dichtung.
      Berlin, 1947.

      Typewritten study on names in the works of
      Thomas Mann; available at the Thomas-Mann-
      Archiv, Zürich.

77   Bartsch, Karl Friedrich
      "Die Eigennamen in Wolframs Parzival und
      Titurel," _Germanistische Studien, Supple-_
      ment Germania. 2 vols. Wien, Gerold, 1875.

      See pp. 114-59 on proper names in "Parzival"
      and "Titurel" by Wolfram.

78   Baskakov, Nikolai Aleksandrovich
      "K etimologii poloveckich sobstvennych imen
      v 'Slove o polku Igoreve'," in _Problemy_
      istorii i dialektologii slavjanskij jazykov.
      Sbornik statej k 70-letiju člena-korrespondenta
      AN SSSR V. I. Borkovskogo. Moskva, Nauka, 1971.

      A Festschrift. On names in the Russian epic
      poem "Igor," see pp. 38-45.

79   Bass, Alfred
        Deutsche Vornamen. Mit Stammwörterbuch.
        Leipzig, Deutsche Zukunft, 1909.

        On German first names; also a dictionary
        of German root words. See also his "Beiträge
        zur Kenntnis deutscher Vornamen," Leipzig,
        Ficker, 1903.

80   Bass, Eben Edward
        "Henry James and the English Country House,"
        Markham Review, 2 (February 1970), 4-10.

81   Bawcutt, N. W.
        "Chapman's Friar Comolet," Notes and Queries,
        15 (1968), 250-2.

82   Bayley, Vernon (Mrs.)
        "The Birth of the Name Shake-Speare,"
        Baconiana, 28 (January 1944), 16-8.

        Refers also to Spenser's "The Faerie Queen."

83   Beadle, Muriel
        "The Game of the Name," The New York Times
        Magazine, (October 21, 1973), 38-9, and 120-32.

        On first names. Refers also to names in novels,
        films, etc.

84   Beatty, C. J. P.
        "Two Noble Families in Hardy's 'The Return of the
        Native'," Notes and Queries, 23 (1976), 402-3.

85   Becker, Henrik
        "Kritisches Namenverzeichnis zum Krimhildlied,"
        Wissenschaftliche Zeitschrift der Friedrich-
        Schiller-Universität Jena. Gesellschafts- und
        Sprachwissenschaftliche Reihe, 5 (1955-6),
        709-26.

        A critical index of the names in the "Krimhild-
        lied."

86   Beckers, Hartmut
      "Horst und Horsa. Ein namenkundliches Problem
      bei Klopstock und in der älteren deutschen
      historiographischen Literatur," Beiträge
      zur Namenforschung, 8 (1973), 13-25.

      On tracing above names in Klopstock's work
      and in Germanic literature in general.

87   Beegle, D. M.
      "Proper Names in the New Isaiah Scroll,"
      American Schools of Oriental Research Bulletin,
      123 (1951), 26-30.

88   Behrend, Fritz
      "Die Namen bei Fontane," Zeitschrift für Bücher-
      freunde, 14 (1922), 39-44.

      See also his Theodor Fontane; zu seinem Leben
      und Schaffen. Berlin, Aldus, 1933. See pp.
      19-34 on names by Fontane.

89   Beiträge zur Theorie und Geschichte der Eigennamen.
      Materialien der namenkundlichen Arbeitstagung
      'Name, Geschichte, kulturelles Erbe', Karl-Marx-
      Universität, Leipzig, 23 und 24-10-1974. Hrsg.
      von dem Zentralinstitut für Sprachwissenschaft,
      Berlin, Akademie der DDR, 1976. (Linguistische
      Studien, No. 30)

      On the theory and history of proper names.

90   Bell, W. Y.
      "Nomenclature and Spanish Literary Analysis,"
      College Language Association Journal, 18 (1974),
      69-80.

      Bellmann, Günter
      See: 1052.

91   Belson, Joel Jay
      The Names in "The Faerie Queene." Columbia
      University, 1964.

      A dissertation on Spenser's work.

92   Beneš, Josef
     "Osobni jména v Jiráskově dile," <u>Obežnik
     kruhu přátel českého jazyka</u>, 20 (December
     15, 1951).

     On names by Jirásek.

93   ---, "Zu Max Brods Namendeutungen," <u>Beiträge zur
     Namenforschung</u>, 4 (1969), 215-6.

     On names by Kafka and others.

94   Bennett, Mildred R.
     "How Willa Cather Chose her Names," <u>Names</u>,
     10 (1962), 29-37.

     Benseler, G.
         See: 882.

     Bentley, E. R. Noel
         See: Noel-Bentley, E. R.

     Beneviste, Emile
         See: 756.

95   Berend, Eduard
     "Die Namengebung bei Jean Paul," <u>Publications
     of the Modern Language Association</u>, 57 (1942),
     820-50.

     On names by Richter.

96   Bergdal, Ed.
     "Hamlet's Name," <u>Scandinavian Studies and Notes</u>
     10 (1929), 159-75.

     On the naming of Shakespeare's Hamlet. Also
     on the names of characters in similar works.

     Berger, Dieter
         See: 39.

     Berger, Jennifer
         See: 1008.

97   Bergmann, Karl
          "Familien- und Vornamen in ihrer Wirkung
          auf Geist und Seele des Menschen,"
          Zeitschrift für Deutschkunde, 48 (1934),
          75-80, and 115-9.

          On the influence of family and first names
          on people. See also for literary names,
          passim.

98   Bergmann, Rolf
          Studien zur Enstehung und Geschichte der
          deutschen Passionsspiele des 13. und 14.
          Jahrhunderts, 1972. (Münstersche Mittelalter-
          Schriften, 14)

          See particularly pp. 243-5 on the name "Rufus"
          in above German passion plays.

99   Beringause, Arthur F.
          "Faulkner's Yoknapatawpha Register," Bucknell
          Review, 11 (1963), 71-82.

100   ---, "Introduction (to Special Issue on 'Names in
          Literature')," Names, 16 (1968), 309-11.

101   ---, "Shmuel Yosef Agnon's 'Soil of the Land of
          Israel': An Onomastic Examination," Literary
          Onomastics Studies, 2 (1975), 1-33.

102   Berman, Peggy Ruth
          French Names for the Dance to 1588. University
          of Pennsylvania, 1968.

          A dissertation.

103   Bernelle, A.
          "Tolstoi ou Tolstoy?" Vie et Langage (1963),
          201-2.

          On the spelling of Tolstoi's name.

104 Bernet-Kempers, August Johan
         Voornamen. Hoe kommen we eraan? Wat doen we
         ermee? Utrecht, Spectrum, 1966. (Prisma
         Boeken, 1133)

         On the history of first names.

105 Berr, Samuel
         An Etymological Glossary to the Old Saxon
         "Heliand." Bern, Lang, 1971. (European
         University Papers, Series I: German Language
         and Literature, Vol. 33)

106 Bertelsen, H.
         Faellesnavne og egennavne. København, Hagerup,
         1911. (Selskab for Germansk Filologi, Smaskrifter
         Nr. 16)

         On proper names.

107 Bertram, Ernst
         Studien zu Adalbert Stifters Novellentechnik.
         Dortmund, Ruhfus, 1907.

         On names in the works of A. Stifter, see pp.
         75-6; see also 2nd edition, 1966, p. 49.

108 Beshevliev, Veselin
         Untersuchungen über die Personennamen bei den
         Thrakern. Amsterdam, Hakkert, 1970.

         On Thracian personal names.

109 ---, Zur Deutung der Kastellnamen in Prokops Werk
         "De Aedificiis." Amsterdam, Hakkert, 1970.

         On names by Caesarea of Procopius.

110 Betz, Werner
         "A Review of Krien's 'Namenphysiognomik ...,"
         Beiträge zur Namenforschung, 12 (1977), 107.

     ---, See: 631.

111   ---, "A Review of Tyroff's 'Namen bei Thomas Mann ...',"
Beiträge zur Namenforschung, 12 (1977), 197.

    ---, See: 1227.

112   Bhatia, Kamala
"Names in Sanskrit Literature," Literary Onomastics Studies, 4 (1977), 1-16.

113   Bierhaus, E. G.
"Strangers in a Room: A Delicate Balance Revis-
ited," Modern Drama, 17 (1974), 199-206.

On names in Albee's drama.

114   Bijur, George
"Boccaccio's Dante," The Times Literary Supplement
(November 4, 1965), 1-3.

115   Binder, Wolfgang
"Hölderlins Namenssymbolik," Hölderlin Jahrbuch,
15 (1961-2), 95-204.

On the symbolism of names in the works of
Hölderlin.

116   Binz, G.
"Zeugnisse zur germanischen Sage in England,"
Beiträge, 20, 144.

On proof of Germanic heroic literature in
England.

    Boschoff, Karl
See: 1052.

117   Bitton, Livia E.
"Biblical Names of Literary Jewesses," Names, 21
(1973), 103-9.

On names of literary heroines.

118 ---, "The Names of the Wandering Jew," <u>Literary Onomastics Studies</u>, 2 (1975), 169-80.

On the variations of the name "Ahasuerus."

119 Björkman, Erik
<u>Studien über die Eigennamen im Beowulf</u>. Halle, 1920. (Studien zur englischen Philologie, 58)

On names in "Beowulf."

120 Blaisdell, Foster W.
"Ívens Saga: Names, "<u>Scandinavian Studies</u>, 41 (1969), 30-40.

121 ---, "Names in the Erex Saga," <u>Journal of English and Germanic Philology</u>, 62 (1963), 143-54.

122 Blatt, T. B.
"Who was Volpone's Danish Gonswart?" <u>English Studies</u>, 56 (1975), 393-5.

On the above name by Ben Jonson.

123 Blenner-Hassett, Roland
<u>A Study of the Place-Names in Lawman's "Brut."</u> Harvard University, 1940.

A dissertation.

124 Bliss, A. J.
"The Hero's Name in the Middle English Version of Lanval," <u>Medium Aevum</u>, 27 (1958), 80-5.

125 Bloom, Edward, A.
"Symbolic Names in Johnson's Periodical Essays," <u>Modern Language Quarterly</u>, 13 (1952), 333-52.

On Names by S. Johnson.

126 Bloom, Leonard
     "Basque Nicknames and Related Onomastic Examples
     in Pío Baroja's Novels," Literary Onomastics
     Studies, 4 (1977), 17-32.

127 Bloomfield, Morton W.
     "Beowulf and Christian Allegory. An Interpreta-
     tion of Unferth," Traditio, 7 (1949-50), 410-5.

128 Boas, Eduard
     Namen-Symbolik der deutschen Poesie. Landsberg,
     Schulz, 1840. (Literaturstoffe, Heft 1)

     On German literary onomastics from the Nibelungen
     to E. T. A. Hoffmann.

     Böckmann, Paul
     See: 1003.

129 Bodelsen, Carl A.
     "The Physiognomy of the Name," A Review of
     English Literature, 2 (1961), 39-48.

     On names mainly by Dickens.

130 Boesch, Bruno
     "Deutsche Namenkunde. Ein Bericht über Neuer-
     scheinungen der letzten Jahre," Wirkendes Wort,
     7 (1956), 1-13.

     A bibliographic report on German onomastics.

131 ---, "Die Eigennamen in ihrer geistigen und seelischen
     Bedeutung für den Menschen," Deutschunterricht,
     9 (1957), 32-50.

     On the meaning of proper names.

132 ---, "Die Namenwelt in Wittenwillers 'Ring' und seinen
     Quellen," Namenforschung. Festschrift für Adolf
     Bach zum 75. Geburtstag am 31. January 1965.
     Hrsg. von Rudolf Schützeichel und Matthias Zender.
     Heidelberg, Winter, 1965.

     See pp. 127-59 on names and sources in Witten-
     weiler's "Ring."

133 ---, "Über die Namengebung mittelhochdeutscher
     Dichter," <u>Deutsche Vierteljahrsschrift für Lite-
     raturwissenschaft und Geistesgeschichte</u>, 32 (1958),
     241-63.

     On names in the works of Middle High German
     writers.

134 Bogle, Edra
     "Personal Names in the Novels of Hermann Hesse,"
     in <u>Love and Wrestling, Butch and O. K.</u> Ed. by F.
     Tarpley. Commerce, Texas, Names Institute Press,
     1973. (South Central Names Institute Publica-
     tion No. 2)

     See pp. 79-84.

135 Bohling, B.
     "Why Michael Henchard?" <u>English Journal</u>, 55
     (1966), 203-7.

     On Hardy's coinage of names.

136 Bojcun, Anna M.
     "Literary Onomastics of Contemporary Slavic
     Novels," <u>Literary Onomastics Studies</u>, 2 (1975),
     141-59.

     On names by Solzhenitsyn, Osadchyi, and Romanski.

137 Bolisani, E.
     "Vergilius o Virgilius? L'opinione di un dotto
     umanista," <u>Atti Ist. Veneto di Scienze, Lettere
     e Arti. Classe di Scienze Morali e Lettere</u>, 117
     (1958-9), 131-41.

     On the spelling of Vergil's name.

138 Bonsdroff, Ingrid von
     "Hankyn or Haukyn?" <u>Modern Philology</u>, 26
     (August 1928), 57-61.

     On spelling variations in "Piers Plowman."

Bonser, Wilfrid
   See: 1152.

139 Borgojakov, M. M.
        "Etničeskie i geografičeskie nazvanija v enisej-
        skih pamjatnikah drevnetjurkskoj pis'mennosti,"
        Učenyje zapiski, 14 Ser. filol. Abakan, 1 (1970),
        77-94.

        On ethnic and geographical denominations in old
        Turkic literature.

Borkovskii, V. I.
   See: 78.

140 Bourazan, Francis
        A Sacred Dictionary. An Explanation of Scripture
        Names and Terms with Brief Geographical and
        Historical References. London, Nisbet, 1890.

Bouteron, Marcel
   See: 698.

141 Bowle, J.
        "Orthography of Shakespeare's Name," The Gentle-
        man's Magazine, 54 (Part I, April 1784), 253-4.

142 Bowman, Walter J.
        "The Titles of Dramatic Works: Problems for
        Translators," Literary Onomastics Studies, 2
        (1975), 181-90.

        On the difficulty of translating names in titles.

143 Bowman, William Dodgson
        The Story of Surnames. London, Routledge, 1932.
        Reprint: Detroit, Gale, 1968.

144 Boyet, Aggie
        "Characterizing Phrases Used in Hawthorne's
        Fiction," in Of Edsels and Marauders. Ed. by
        F. Tarpley and A. Moseley. Commerce, Texas,
        Names Institute Press, 1971. (South Central
        Names Institute Publication No. 1)

        See pp. 82-8.

145 Bradley, Henry, and Mayhew, A. L.
"The Surname 'Shakspere'," The Academy, 31
(February 5, 1887), 94; (March 5, 1887), 168;
(March 12, 1887), 183; (March 19, 1887), 203,
and (March 26, 1887), 222.

146 Bratto, O.
"Molière, les Femmes savantes; Etude d'anthroponymie littéraire, "Revue Internationale
d'Onomastique, 25 (1973), 257-69.

On names by Molière.

147 Braune, Wilhelm
"Otenheim im Nibelungenliede," Beiträge zur
Geschichte der deutschen Sprache und Literatur,
9 (1884), 553-60.

On the name "Otenheim" in the Nibelungen.

148 Bréal, Michel Jules Alfred
Essai de sémantique. Science des significations.
Paris, Hachette, 1907.

See pp. 191-8 on "Comment les noms sont donnés
aux choses." See also the English edition:
Semantics. Studies in the Science of Meaning.
Tr. by H. Cust. New York, 1940. See pp. 171-7 on
"How Names Are Given to Things."

149 Brechenmacher, Josef Karlmann
Etymologisches Wörterbuch der deutschen Familiennamen. 2 vols. Limburg, Starke, 1957-63.

Vol. 1: A-J; Vol. 2: K-Z. An etymological
dictionary of German family names.

Brée, Germaine
See: 815.

150 Brewer, E. C.
The Reader's Handbook of Famous Names in Fiction,
References, Proverbs, Plots, Stories, and Poems.
2. vols. Revised and enlarged edition. Philadel
phia, Lippincott, 1899. Reprint, 1966.

151 Broëns, M.
     "L'Anthroponomie des Sarrasins dans les chansons
     de geste," <u>Kongressberichte</u> (München), 2 (1961),
     169-74.

     On personal names in the chansons de geste.

152 ---, "Ce que révèle l'onomastique des chansons de
     geste des cycles méridionaux," <u>VI. Internationa-
     ler Kongress für Namenforschung</u> (München), 1958,
     55.

     On names in the chasons de geste.

153 Brown, Calvin S.
     "Odysseus and Polyphemus: The Name and the
     Curse," <u>Comparative Literature</u>, 18 (Summer
     1966), 193-202.

     On the power of the above names by Homer.

154 Brown, K.
     "Polonius and Fortinbras (and Hamlet?)" <u>English
     Studies</u>, 55 (1974), 218-38.

   Brown, Richard A.
     See: 232.

155 Bruce, John
     "On the Orthography of Shakspere, "<u>The Gentel-
     man's Magazine</u>, 167 (February 1840), 161-6;
     (April 1840), 374-9; (June 1840), 591-4.

156 Brueva, E. M.
     "Funkcija ličnych imen v sovetskoj basne,"
     <u>Onomastika Povolž'ja</u>, 2 (1971), 327-31.

     On the functions of proper names in Soviet
     fables.

157 Brumbaugh, T. B.
     "Macaulay and Niebuhr (Pronunciation of Porsena),"
     <u>Notes and Queries</u>, 19 (1972), 408.

158 Buchan, John
        Literature and Topography. Homilies and Recrea
        tions. Boston, Houghton, 1926. Reprint: Free
        port, Books for Libraries Series, 1969.

        Originally an address to the Working Men's
        College, London, February 20, 1926. From Greek
        and Latin poets' to Hardy's use of names.
        See pp. 181-206.

    Buchanan, George
        See: 790.

159 Buchwald, W.
        "A Review of D. C. E. Swanson's 'The Names in
        Roman Verse'," Gnomon, 41 (1969), 507-9.

    ---, See: 1182.

    Bučko, A. E. Lopušanskaja
        See: Lopušanskaja-Bučko, A. E.

160 Budimir, M.
        "De Iliade quadam Phrygia," Živa Antika (Skopje
        8 (1958), 227-35.

        On names by Homer.

161 Büky, Béla
        "Namengebrauch - Namengebung. Funktionsparal-
        lelismus zwischen Eigennamen und Adjektiven,"
        Beiträge zur Namenforschung, 11 (1976), 361-74

        On parallelism of proper names and adjectives.

    Buma, W. J.
        See: 1021.

162 Burelbach, Frederick M.
        "Two Family Names: Faulkner and Sartoris,"
        Literary Onomastics Studies, 4 (1977), 81-96.

Burger, Harald
    See: 1056.

163 Burgess, Gelett
    "Make a Name for Yourself," The Saturday Review
    of Literature, 30 (January 25, 1947), 9-10, and
    41.

    On how to coin names.

164 Burgon, John William
    "On the Orthography of Shakspeare," The Gentle-
    man's Magazine, 167 (May 1840), 474-80.

165 ---, "'Shakspeare' the Received Orthography Vindica-
    ted," The Gentleman's Magazine, 167 (March 1840),
    264-7.

    Burgstahler, Th.
      See: 1049.

166 Burke, James F.
    "Names and the Significance of Etymology in the
    'Libro del Cavallero Cifar'," The Romanic Review,
    59 (October 1968), 161-73.

    On names by Cifar.

167 Buyssens, E.
    "Du nom propre et du nom commun," Neophilologus,
    23 (1938), 111-21.

    On proper and common names.

Caffee, Nathaniel M.
See: 507.

Carney, James
See: 864.

168 Carpenter, Stanley S.
The Appropriate Name in the "Bucolics"
of Vergil. University of Illinois at
Urbana Champaign, 1943.

A dissertation.

Carrington, Constance Mary Matthews
See: Matthews, Constance Mary Carrington

Cascorbi, Paul
See: 464.

169 Cassirer, Ernst
Philosophie der symbolischen Formen.
3 vols. Berlin, Cassirer, 1923-9.

See also the English edition: The
Philosophy of Symbolic Form. Trans-
lated by Ralph Manheim. 3 vol. New
Haven, Yale University Press, 1955.
See Vol. 2, pp. 40-51, on "Myth and
Name."

170 Causse, Rolande, and Jaques Le Scanff
Le grand livre des prénoms. Paris, Hachette,
1972.

On French personal names.

171 Century Cyclopedia of Names. A pronouncing
and etymological dictionary of names in
geography, biography, mythology, history,
ethnology, art, archeology, fiction, etc.
Ed. by Benjamin E. Smith. New York, Century,
1894.

172   Century Dictionary and Cyclopedia. With a new
           atlas of the world; a work of general ref-
           erence in all departments of knowledge.
           Revised and enlarged edition. 12 vols.
           New York, Century, 1911.

           See Vol. 11: The Century Cyclopedia of
           Names. Ed. by Benjamin E. Smith.

173   Černjaeva, V. M.
           "Sobstvennye imena v revoljucionno-
           demokratičeskoj stichotvornoj satire
           60-h 1. XIX veka," Onomastika Povolž'ja,
           2 (1971), 315-8.

           On proper names in Russian political satire
           of the 1860s.

174   Cerny, James W.
           "Joyce's Mental Map," James Joyce Quarterly,
           9 (Winter 1971), 218-24.

           On names of rivers in "Finnegan's Wake."
           See also his "Unfolding a Mental Map,"
           Monadnock, 47 (1973), 31-42.

175   Chajes, Hirsch Perez
           Beiträge zur nordsemitischen Onomatologie.
           Wien, Gerold, 1900. (Kaiserliche Akademie
           der Wissenschaften. Sitzungsberichte.
           Philosophisch-historische Klasse, Bd. 143)

           On North Semitic onomatology.

176   Chamberlin, Vernon A.
           "The Significance of the Name 'Almudena' in
           Galdós's 'Misericordia'," Hispania, 47 (1964),
           491-6.

177   Chambers, Edmund Kerchever
           William Shakespeare; A Study of Facts and
           Problems. 2 vols. Oxford, Clarendon, 1930.

           On the name of Shakespeare, see Vol. 2,
           pp. 354-76.

-29-

178 Chambers, Frank M.
Proper Names in the Lyrics of the Trouba-
dours. Chapel Hill, University of North
Carolina Press, 1971. (Studies in the
Romance Languages and Literatures No. 113)

179 Chambers, Robert
The Book of Days. A miscellany of popular
antiquities in connection with the calendar,
including anecdotes, biography, & history,
curiosities of literature and oddities of
human life and character. 2 vols.
Edinburgh, Chambers, 1863-4.

On rhythmic puns on names including Shakespeare's, see Vol. 1, pp. 65-7.

180 Chambers, William
"On Spelling the Name of Shakespeare,"
The European Magazine, 64 (July, 1813), 23.

181 Champion, Larry S.
"Shakespeare's 'Nell'," Names, 16 (1968),
357-61.

182 Chandler, Alice
"Name Symbolism of Captain Vere," 19th
Century Fiction, 22 (1967), 86-9.

On the above name by Melville.

183 Chapman, Coolidge Otis
An Index of Names in Pearl, Purity,
Patience, and Gawain. Ithaca, Cornell
University Press, 1951. (Cornell Studies
in English, Vol. 38)

On names in Middle English poems.

184 Chapman, Robert William
        "Proper Names in Poetry," in The Portrait
        of a Scholar, and Other Essays Written in
        Macedonia, 1916-8. London, Oxford, 1920.

        See pp. 23-8.

185 ---, "A Reply to Watt's Study on Defoe,
        Richardson, and Fielding," Review of
        English Studies, 1 (1950), 252.

        ---, See: 1271.

186 Chard, L. F.
        "Jane Austen and the Obituaries: The Names
        of Northanger Abbey," Studies in the Novel,
        7 (1975), 133-6.

187 Chase, G. D.
        "The Origin of the Roman Praenomina,"
        Harvard Studies in Classical Philology,
        8 (1897), 103-84.

188 Chessex, Pierre
        Origine des noms de personnes: sens et
        origine des prénoms, des noms de famille
        et des surnoms. Lausanne, Guilde du livre,
        1946. (Collection Gal savoir, Vol. 12)

        On French personal names; on the origin of
        family names and surnames.

189 Chiba, M.
        "Shinkokinshū ni okeru chimei uta," Nihon
        Bungaku Nōto/Japanese Literary Notes, 5 (1970).

        On names in the Japanese anthology of
        Shinkokinshū.

190 Childers, W. C.
        "Edwin Arlington Robinson's Proper Names,"
        Names, 3 (1955), 223-9.

191 Christmann, Ernst
"Kriemhilde in pfälzischen Flurnamen,"
Beiträge zur Namenforschung, 4 (1969),
376-9.

On toponyma in Kriemhilt.

192 ---, "'Reinhard' der Fuchs und 'Gerhard'
der Gänsereich - Wie kamen Tiere zu
solchen Menschennamen?" Hessische
Blätter für Volkskunde, 41 (1950),
100-17.

On animal names.

Churchill, Thomas W.
See: 530.

193 Clark, G. A.
"Proper Nouns in Logic and Literature,"
Journal of Philosophy, 58 (1961), 690-1.

On names by Dickens.

194 Clark, P. O.
"A Reply to R. M. Smith's Study on Names
by Swift," Journal of English and Germanic
Philology, 56 (1957), 154-62.

---, See: 1117.

195 Clark, Roy Peter
"A Possible Pun on Chaucer's Name," Names,
25 (1977), 49-50.

196 Clodd, Edward
Magic in Names and Other Things. London,
Chapman, 1920.

On names, general.

197 Coard, Robert L.
     "Names in the Fiction of Edith Wharton,"
     Names, 13 (1965), 1-10.

198 ---, "Names in the Fiction of Sinclair Lewis,"
     Georgia Review, 16 (1962), 318-29.

199 Coates, Richard A.
     "A Personal Name Etymology and a Shakes-
     pearean Dramatic Motiv," Names, 24 (1976),
     1-8.

200 Cochran, R.
     "Babo's Name in Benito Cereno: An Unneces-
     sary Controversy?" American Literature,
     48 (1976), 217-9.

     On the above name by Melville.

201 Coffeen, Robert Gene
     Naming Techniques in Whitman's "Leaves of
     Grass." A Study in Problems of Power.
     University of North Carolina at Chapel Hill,
     1969.

     A dissertation.

202 Cohen, K.
     "Note on Milton's Azazel," Philological
     Quarterly, 49 (1970), 248-9.

203 Cohen, L. H.
     "What's in a Name? The Presence of the
     Victim in 'The Pioneers'," Massachusetts
     Review, 16 (1975), 688-98.

     On names in James Fenimore Cooper's novel.

204 Cohn, Robert Greer
     "Wherefore Igitur," The Romanic Review, 60
     (1969), 174-7.

     On names by Mallarmé.

205   Coleman, A. F.
        <u>Humor in the Russian Comedy from Catherine</u>
        <u>to Gogol</u>. New York, Columbia University
        Press, 1925.

        On Russian literary onomastics, see p. 5,
        passim.

206   Colwell, James L.
        "Huckleberries and Humans: On the Naming
        of Huckleberry Finn," <u>Publications of the</u>
        <u>Modern Language Association</u>, 86 (1971), 70-6.

        On the above name by M. Twain.

207   Conley, J.
        "Peculiar Name 'Thopas'," <u>Studies in</u>
        <u>Philology</u>, 73 (1976), 42-61.

        On the above name by Chaucer.

208   Conner, Lester Irvin
        <u>A Yeats Dictionary: Names of the Persons</u>
        <u>and Places in the Poetry of W. B. Yeats</u>.
        New York, Columbia University, 1964.

        A dissertation.

209   Conner, Wayne
        "Balzac's Frenkofer," <u>Modern Language Notes</u>,
        69 (1954), 335-8.

210   ---, <u>Un Aspect de l'onomastique balzacienne:</u>
        <u>l'Élaboration des noms de personnage</u>. Presse
        de l'Université Laval, 1976. (Actes de XIIIe
        Congrès International de Linguistique et
        Philologie Romanes, Vol. 1)

        On Balzac's names. See particularly
        pp. 943-51.

211   Connolly, T. E.
        "Note on Name-Symbolism in Melville,"
        <u>American Literature</u>, 25 (1954), 489-90.

212 Coogan, Michael David
West Semitic Personal Names in the
Murasu Documents. Harvard University,
1971.

A dissertation.

213 Cook, George A.
"Names in 'The American'," College English
Association, 28 (April 1966), 5.

On names by H. James.

214 Corbett, Frederick St. John
A History of British Poetry. London, Gay,
1904.

On the orthography of Shakespeare's name,
see Appendix II, pp. 616-9.

215 Corney, Bolton
"On the Authograph of Shakespeare," The
Gentleman's Magazine, 167 (April 1840),
379-80.

216 Corson, Hiram
An Introduction to the Study of Shakespeare.
Boston, Heath, 1893.

On the spelling of Shakespeare's name, see
pp. 358-60.

217 ─ ─, Index of Proper Names and Subjects to Chaucer's
"Canterbury Tales." London, Oxford, 1911 for
1884. (Chaucer Society Publication, 1st
Series, No. 72)

218 Coseriu, Eugenio
Sprachtheorie und allgemeine Sprachwissenschaft. Tr. by Uwe Petersen. München, Fink,
1975. (Internationale Bibliothek für allgemeine Linguistik, Bd. 2)

See pp. 234-52 on the theory of proper names.
See also original edition: Teoria del lenguaje
y linguistica general, Madrid, 1962.

---, See: 1051.

219 Cottrell, Allan P.
    "The Significance of the Name 'Johannes'
    in 'Die Judenbuche'," Seminar, VI/3 (1970),
    207-15.

    On the above name by Annette von Droste-
    Hülshoff.

220 Cowser, Robert L.
    "The Significance of Certain Names in
    Langston Hughes' Fiction," in They Had to
    Call It Something. Ed. by F. Tarpley.
    Commerce, Texas, Names Institute Press,
    1974. (South Central Names Institute
    Publication No. 3)

    See pp. 111-4.

221 ---, "Symbolic Names in the Plays of Tennessee
    Williams," in Of Edsels and Marauders.
    Ed. by F. Tarpley and A. Moseley. Commerce,
    Texas, Names Institute Press, 1971.
    (South Central Names Institute Publica-
    tion No. 1)

    See pp. 89-93.

222 Crab, Timothy
    "Shakespeare's Name," The Gentleman's
    Magazine, 57 (March 1787), 204.

    Crawford, Thomas
    See: 1071.

    Creed, Howard
    See: 976.

223 Cristureanu, Al
    "Imagini livresti formate din numele
    proprii in opera lui Costache Negruzzi,"
    Limba si Literatura, 21 (1969), 151-7.

    On proper names in the works of C. Negruzzi.

224   Cross, A. E. Brookes
            "Names in Dickens and Elsewhere," The
            Dickensian, 22 (April-June 1926), 129-30.

225   Crozier, R. D.
            "Home James: Hemingway's 'Jacob'," Papers
            on Language and Literature, 11 (1975),
            293-301.

226   Crum, Earl Le Verne
            Index of Proper Names in Servius. Univer-
            sity of Iowa, 1927. (Humanistic Studies,
            Vol. 4, No. 1)

227   Cunningham, Everett V.
            "Bleibtreu in Joyce's Ulysses," Names,
            1 (1953), 203-4.

228   Curtiss, Philip
            "When is a Ford not a Ford?" Harper's
            Monthly Magazine, 145 (August 1922),
            407-10.

            On real and imaginary names in literature.

229   Curtius, Ernst Robert
            Europäische Literatur und lateinisches
            Mittelalter. Bern, Francke, 1948. New
            edition: 1976.

            See "Etymologie als Denkform," pp. 488-92.
            See also English edition: European Liter-
            ature and the Latin Middle Ages. Translated
            By Willard R. Trask. New York, Pantheon,
            1953. (Bollingen Series, 36) See pp.
            495-500: "Etymology as a Category of
            Thought."

        Cust, H.
            See: 148.

230 Cyplenkova, L. H.
        "Upotreblenie imen sobstvennych v sovre-
        mennoj poezii," in Naučnaja konferencija
        molodych učenych, Adygen, 1969; Majkop,
        1970. (Doklady i soobščenija, 1)

        On proper names in contemporary Russian
        poetry, see pp. 177-82.

231 Czeglédy, K.
        "Oszmán apósa Anonymusnál?" Magyar Nyelv,
        55 (1959), 519.

        On the name "Eunedubelianus" in the works
        of the Hungarian poet Anonymus.

232 Dacus, Lee, and Richard A. Brown
        "Some Names in the Legend and Ballad
        of 'Tom Dooley'," in Naughty Names.
        Ed. by F. Tarpley. Commerce, Texas,
        Names Institute Press, 1975. (South
        Central Names Institute Publication
        No. 4)

        See pp. 35-8.

233 Darsavelidze, N.
        "Zamečanija o sobstvennych imenach v
        'Amirandaredžaniani'," Jubilejnyj
        sbornik, posvjascennyj B. S. Ahvledinai
        v svjazi s 80-letiem so dnja roždenija.
        Tbilisi, 1969.

        A Festschrift. On names in above medieval
        Georgian poem, see pp. 362-8.

234 Dash, Irene G.
        "Bohemia's 'Sea Coast' and the Babe Who
        Was 'Lost Forever'," Literary Onomastics
        Studies, 3 (1976), 102-9.

        On names in the works of Shakespeare.

     da Silva, Fontes Henrique
        See: Fontes, Henrique da Silva

235 Dauzat, Albert
        Dictionnaire étymologique des noms de
        famille et prénoms de France. Paris,
        Larousse, 1955.

        On French personal names.

236 ---, Les noms de personnes, origine et évolution;
        prénoms - noms de famille - surnoms -
        pseudonymes. Paris, Delagrave, 1925.

        On French personal names. See also later
        edition.

237　Davis, Catherine W.
　　　　1001 First Names from Stage and Screen,
　　　　Life and Literature. Peoria, Henniges,
　　　　1942.

238　Davis, Charles Edward
　　　　Eudora Welty's Art of Naming. Emory Uni-
　　　　versity, 1969.

　　　　A dissertation.

239　Debrabandere, F.
　　　　"Voornamen uit de ridderliteratuur,"
　　　　Leiegouw, 11 (1969), 277-87.

　　　　On names in Flemish chivalry literature.

240　Debus, F. L.
　　　　Aspekte zum Verhältnis Name-Wort.
　　　　Groningen, Wolters, 1966.

　　　　An analysis of "nomen proprium" and
　　　　"appellativum."

241　DeGraaff, Robert V.
　　　　"Meredith's Use of Names in 'The Ordeal
　　　　of Richard Feverel'," 9. Supplement to
　　　　the Bulletin of the American Name Society,
　　　　44 (1976), 1-5.

　　　d'Heylii, G.
　　　　See: Heylii, G. d'

242　D'Isaeli, Isaac
　　　　"The Orthography of Shakespeare," The
　　　　Gentleman's Magazine, 167 (January 1840),
　　　　39-40.

　　　de Keyser, P.
　　　　See: Keyser, P. de

　　　de Laski, E.
　　　　See: Laski, E. de

243 Demetz, Peter
     Formen des Realismus: Theodor Fontane.
     Kritische Untersuchungen. München, Hanser,
     1964. (Literatur als Kunst)

     See pp. 193-203: "Zur Rhetorik Fontanes.
     Die Kunst der Namen." On names by Fontane.

244 ---, "Notes on Figurative Names in Theodor
     Fontane's Novels," The Germanic Review,
     37 (1962), 96-105.

de Rochetal, A.
     See: Rochetal, A. de

de Silva, Guido Gómez
     See: Gómez de Silva, Guido

de Vajay, S.
     See: Vajay, S. de

de Vries, J.
     See: Vries, J. de

de Weever, J. E.
     See: Weever, J. E. de

Dickenmann, Ernst
     See: 1054.

245 Dilke, O. A. W.
     "Metrical Treatment of Proper Names in
     Statius," Classical Review, 63 (1949),
     50-1.

246 Dillard, J. L.
     Black Names. The Hague, Mouton, 1976.
     (Contributions to Sociology of Language,
     13)

     Includes a chapter on personal names.

247 Dillon, Bert
     A Chaucer Dictionary. Proper Names and
     Allusions. Excluding Place Names. Boston,
     Hall, 1974.

248 ---, A Dictionary of Personal, Mythological,
     Allegorical, and Astrological Proper Names
     and Allusions in the Works of Geoffrey
     Chaucer. Duke University, 1972.

     A dissertation.

249 Dittmaier, Heinrich
     "Ursprung und Geschichte der deutschen
     Satznamen. Zugleich ein Beitrag zur
     vergleichenden Namenkunde," Rheinisches
     Jahrbuch für Volkskunde, 7 (1956), 7-94.

     On the origin and the history of German
     sentence names.

250 Dixon, Benjamin Homer
     Surnames. Boston, Wilson, 1855.

     See also supplement to 1858.

251 Dmitriev, V.
     "Pod vymyšlennymi imenami," Russkaja reč,
     3 (1969), 15-20.

     On Russian literary onomastics.

     ---, See: 861.

252 Doer, Bruno
     Die römische Namengebung. Ein historischer
     Versuch. Stuttgart, Kohlhammer, 1937.

     On Roman names; a historical approach.

253 ---, Untersuchungen zur römischen Namengebung.
     Berlin, 1937.

     A dissertation on Roman names.

254 Dolan, J. R.
     English Ancestral Names. The Evolution of
     the Surname from Medieval Occupations. New
     York, Potter, 1972.

     On English personal names.

255 Doran, Linda Kay Dyer
     Naming as Disclosure: A Study of Theme
     and Method in the Fiction of Walker Percy.
     George Peabody College for Teachers, 1976.

     A dissertation.

     Doren, Carl Van
     See: Van Doren, Carl

256 Dornseiff, Franz
     "Redende Namen," Zeitschrift für Namenfor-
     schung, 16 (1940), 24-38, and 215-8.

     On literary onomastics from Greek classics
     to German writers; mainly on descriptive
     names.

257 Douglas, George
     "A Gossip About Novelists' Names,"
     Chambers's Journal, 97 (September 1920),
     671-2.

     On coinage of names in novels.

258 Dow, Eddy
     "H. James' 'Brooksmith' (Paragraphs 4 and
     5)," Explicator, 27 (January 1969), 35.

259 Dragos, Elena
     "Functia simbolică a imaginii in romanul
     lui Liviu Rebreanu," Studia Universitatis
     Babes-Bólyai Philosophia, 17 (1972), 37-44.

     On names in the novels by Rebreanu.

     Dravina, Velta Rūke
     See: Rūke-Dravina, Velta

260   Drosdowski, Günther
        Lexikon der Vornamen. Herkunft, Bedeutung
        und Gebrauch von mehr als 3000 Vornamen.
        Mannheim, Bibliographisches Institut, 1968.
        (Duden-Taschenbücher, Bd. 4)

        A lexicon of first names.

        du Gard, Rene Coulet
        See: Gard, Rene Coulet du

261   Duncan-Jones, E. E.
        "A Reply to Watt's Study on Names by Defoe,
        Richardson, and Fielding," Review of English
        Studies, N. S. 1, (1950), 252.

        ---, See: 1271.

262   Duncan, Robert M.
        An Etymological Vocabulary of Plant Names
        in the Works of Alfonso el Sabio.   University
        of Wisconsin, 1936.

        A dissertation.

263   ---, "Names in the Documents lingüísticos
        España," New Mexico Foklore Record, 12
        (1969/70), 12-6.

264   Dunkling, Leslie Alan
        First Names First.   New York, Universe Books,
        1977.

        Refers to names in literature, passim.

265   Durić, M.
        "Značenje izrara 'Radojički' u pesni 'Do
        pojasa' Lace Kostića," Zbornik istorije
        književnosti Sanu (Belgrad), 6 (1970), 71.

        On names by Kostića.

266 Dvonč, L.
"O menách typu Maróthy-Šoltésovej,"
Slovenská reč, 27 (1962), 252-3.

On they types of names by E. Maróthy-
Šoltésová.

267 Eaves, T. C. D., and B. D. Kinpel
           "Two Names in Joseph Andrews," <u>Modern</u>
           <u>Philology</u>, 72 (1975), 408-9.

268 Eckstein, Ernst
           "Wie tauf' ich meine Helden?" in <u>Leichte</u>
           <u>Waare. Literarische Skizzen</u>. Leipzig,
           Hartknoch, 1874.

           See pp. 85-96 on German literary onomastics.

269 Eerde, J. van
           "Importance of Nomenclature in a French
           Classical Comedy," <u>Names</u>, 7 (1959), 271-2.

           On Hauteroche's names.

270 ---, "Names in Some Works of Malaparte," <u>Names</u>,
           6 (1958), 88-96.

271 Eggan, Lloyd Arthur
           <u>On the Thesis That Common Nouns Are Names</u>,
           <u>and the Question of Extension Determination</u>.
           University of Wisconsin, Madison, 1975.

           A dissertation.

272 Egle, K.
           "Druviena Poruku Jāna dailradē," <u>Karogs</u>
           (Riga), 10 (1971), 130-2.

           On names in the works of Jānis Poruks.

273 Egmond, Peter von
           "Naming Techniques in John Galsworthy's
           'The Forsyte Saga'," <u>Names</u>, 16 (1968),
           371-9.

274 Eichler, Ernst, and Hans Walther
           "Name, Geschichte und kulturelles Erbe,"
           <u>Zeitschrift für Phonetik. Sprachwissen-</u>
           <u>schaft und Kommunikationsforschung</u>, 29
           (1976), 98-9.

           On the history of names.

Eifler, Günter
See: 1052.

275 Einarsson, S.
"Beowulfian Place Names in East Iceland,"
Modern Language Notes, 76 (1961), 385-92.

276 Eis, Gerhard
"Die deutschen Vorstufen der Ironsaga,"
Arktiv för nordisk filologi, 67 (1952),
182-97.

On preliminary German elements of the
Iron Saga.

277 ---, "Rufnamen der Tiere," Neophilologus, 48 (1964),
122-46.

On animal names.

278 ---, "Tests über suggestive Personennamen in der
modernen Literatur und im Alltag," Beiträge
zur Namenforschung, 10 (1959), 293-308.

On tests of suggestive names in modern
literature and in the everyday world.

279 ---, Über die Namen im Kriminalroman der
Gegenwart," Neophilologus, 49 (1965),
307-32.

On names in contemporary detective stories.

280 ---, Vom Zauber der Namen. 4 Essays. Berlin,
Schmidt, 1970.

Four essays on the magic of names. It
includes "Tests über suggestive Personennamen ..."; "Rufnamen der Tiere"; "Über die
Namen im Kriminalroman ...", and "Zur
Diskussion über die Namenphysiognomien."

281 ---, "Zur Diskussion über die Namenphysiognomien".

On the physiognomy of names. Also in his
Vom Zauber der Namen.

282 Eliason, Norman E.
"Personal Names in the 'Canterbury Tales',"
Names, 21 (1973), 137-52.

On names by Chaucer.

283 Ellis, Alexander John
"The Pronunciation of Shakespeare's Name,"
The Athenaeum, (Part II, August 17, 1872),
207.

284 Els, T. J. M. van
The Kassel Manuscript of Bede's "Historia
ecclesiastica gentis Anglorum". Assen, van
Gorcum, 1972.

On Anglo-Saxon names by Bede.

285 Elze, Karl
Essays on Shakespeare. Tr. by L. D. Schmitz.
London, Macmillan, 1874.

On Shakespeare's name see pp. 368-79.
Originally contributed to the Jahrbuch der
deutschen Shakespeare Gesellschaft, Weimar.

286 ---, William Shakespeare. Halle, Waisenhaus,
1876.

See also English translation by L. D. Schmitz.
London, Bell, 1901.

Emden, W. G. van
See: Van Emden, W. G.

287 Emrich, Wilhelm
       Franz Kafka. A Critical Study of His
       Writings. Tr. by Sheema Zeben Buehne.
       New York, Ungar, 1968.

       See also the original German edition:
       Franz Kafka. Frankfurt, Athenäum, 1970,
       passim. See particularly discussions of
       Samsa, Gracchus, etc.

288 English, G.
       "On the Psychological Response to Unknown
       Proper Names," The American Journal of
       Psychology, 27 (1916), 430-4.

289 Epstein, E. L.
       "Novels of J. R. R. Tolkien and the
       Ethnology of Medieval Christendom,"
       Philological Quarterly, 48 (1969),
       517-25.

290 Erler, Ernst
       Die Namengebung bei Shakespeare. Heidel-
       berg, Winter, 1913. (Anglistische Arbeiten,
       2)

       On names by Shakespeare.

291 Ermatinger, Emil
       Das dichterische Kunstwerk. Leipzig,
       Teubner, 1921. (Grundbegriffe der
       Urteilsbildung in der Literaturgeschichte)

       On literary onomastics, see pp. 354-5.

292 Etkind, E. G.
       "Motivirovannost' imeni sobstvennogo v
       poetičeskom kontekste," Seminar poproбleme
       motivirovannosti jazykovogo znaka.
       Leningrad, 1969.

       On motivations of Russian names in literary
       context, see "Materialy" pp. 40-3.

293 "Étymologie de Panurge, Raminagrobis, Panta-
       gruel, Harpagon et Purgos," Intermédiaire
       des Chercheurs et Curieux, 19 (1969),
       796-8.

       On the etymology of the above names.

294 Eusebius, Caesariensis
       Das Onomastikon der biblischen Ortsnamen.
       Die griechischen christlichen Schriftsteller
       der ersten drei Jahrhunderte. Leipzig,
       1904. Reprint: New York, Olms, 1966.

       An onomasticon of Biblical toponyma.

295 Ewen, Cecil Henry L'Estrange
       A Guide to the Origin of British Surnames.
       London, Gifford, 1938.

       On English personal names.

296 ---, A History of Surnames of the British Isles.
       A Concise Account of Their Origin, Evolu-
       tion, Etymology, and Legal Status. London,
       Paul, 1931. Reprint, 1968.

       On English personal names.

297 ---, "The Name 'Shakespeare'," Baconiana, 22
       (June 1936), 171-85.

       Refers to "Saxby."

298 ---, "The Name Shakespeare," Notes and Queries,
       171 (1936), 187-8.

299   Fabia, Philipp
      <u>Onomasticon Taciteum</u>. Paris, 1900.   Reprint:
      New York, Olms, 1964.

      An onomasticon on Tacitus.

300   Fabianskaja, V. A.
      "Imena sobstvennyje kak sredstvo tipizacii
      v rasskaze V. G. Korolenko 'Son Makara',
      <u>Respublikanska Onomastyčna Konferencija</u>
      <u>Kyjiv</u>, 4 (1969), 139-40.

      On names by Korolenko.

301   Falk, Walter
      <u>Das Nibelungenlied in seiner Epoche. Re-</u>
      <u>vision eines romantischen Mythos</u>. Heidelberg,
      Winter, 1974. (Germanische Bibliothek. 3.
      Reihe. Untersuchungen und Einzeldarstellun-
      gen)

      On names in the Nibelungen, see pp. 153-9,
      and 198-9.

302   Farber, L.
      "Fading: A Way; Gertrude Stein's Sources
      for Three Lives," <u>Journal of Modern Liter-</u>
      <u>ature</u>, 5 (1976), 463-80.

303   Fatout, Paul
      "Mark Twain's 'Nom de Plume'," <u>American</u>
      <u>Literature</u>, 34 (1962), 1-7.

      On his pen name.

304   Feldman, Thalia Phillies
      "Onomastic Concepts of 'Bear' in Comparative
      Myth: Anglo-Saxon and Greek Literature,"
      <u>Literary Onomastics Studies</u>, 1 (1974), 1-21.

305   ---, "Terminology for 'Kingship and God' in
      'Beowulf'," <u>Literary Onomastics Studies</u>,
      2 (1975), 100-15.

306   Festchrift Adolf Bach. 2 vols. Bonn, Rohrscheid,
      1955-6. (Rheinische Vierteljahrsblätter,
      20-1)

      A collection of essays on names.

307   Fichter, W. L.
      "Probable Sources of Certain Character Names
      Used by Lope de Vega," Hispanic Review, 30
      (1962), 267-74.

308   Fick, August
      Die griechischen Personennamen nach ihrer
      Bildung erklärt und systematisch geordnet.
      Göttingen, Vandenhoeck, 1894.

      On Greek personal names.

309   Fickert, Kurt J.
      "Wit and Wisdom in Dürrenmatt's Names,"
      Contemporary Literature, 11 (Summer 1970),
      382-8.

310   Fiedler, Hermann Georg
      "The Oldest Study of Germanic Proper Names,"
      The Modern Language Review, 37 (April 1942),
      185-92.

311   ──, "Why Goethe Altered Faust's Christian Name,"
      The Modern Language Review, 38 (1943), 347-8.

312   Fiesel, Eva
      Die Sprachphilosophie der deutschen Romantik.
      Tübingen, Mohr, 1927. Reprint: Hildesheim,
      Olms, 1973.

      On names by German romanticists, see pp.
      13-4.

313   Filips, Katherine
      "The Names of Poets in Georgij Ivanov's
      Poetry'," Names, 15 (1967), 70-7.

314 Fingerhut, Karl-Heinz
        Die Funktion der Tierfiguren im Werke Franz
        Kafkas. Offene Erzählgerüste und Figurenspiele.
        Bonn, Bouvier, 1969. (Abhandlungen zur Kunst-,
        und Literaturwissenschaft, Bd. 89)

        On names by Kafka. See particularly pp. 294-5,
        passim.

315 Finnie, W. Bruce
        "The Structural Function of Names in the Works
        of Chrétien de Troyes," Names, 20 (1972), 91-4.

316 Finsterwalder, Karl
        Die Familiennamen in Tirol und Nachbargebieten
        und die Entwicklung des Personennamens im
        Mittelalter. Mit einem urkundlichen Nachschlag-
        werk für 4100 Familien- und Hofnamen. Inns-
        bruck, Wagner, 1951. (Schlern-Schriften, 81)

        On Tirolian personal names and their develop-
        ment in the Middle Ages. See particularly
        p. 26.

---, See: 609, 997, 1175.

Firmat, Maria Lourdes Albertos
     See: Albertos Firmat, Maria Lourdes

317 Fischer, B. P.
        "Phyteus in Marlowe's Tamburlaine," Notes
        and Queries, 22 (1975), 247-8.

318 Fischer, Rudolf
        "Friedrich Engels und die Namenforschung,"
        Wissenschaftliche Zeitschrift der Karl-Marx-
        Universität. Gesellschafts- und sprachwissen-
        schaftliche Reihe (Jena), 4 (1952-3), 25-6.

        Engels and onomastics.

319 ---, Onomastica Slavogermanica. Berlin. Akademie
        Verlag, 1965. (Abhandlungen der sächsischen
        Akademie der Wissenschaften zu Leipzig.
        Philologisch-historische Klasse, Bd. 58)

        A collection of essays on Slavo-Germanic
        names.

320 Fleischer, Wolfgang
        Die deutschen Personennamen; Geschichte,
        Bildung und Bedeutung. Berlin, Akademie,
        1964. (Wissenschaftliche Taschenbücher.
        Reihe Sprachwissenschaft, Bd. 20)

        On German personal names.

321 ---, "Zum Verhältnis von Name und Appellativum in
        Deutschen," Wissenschaftliche Zeitschrift der
        Karl-Marx-Universität, Gesselschafts- und
        Sprachwissenschaftliche Reihe, 13 (1964),
        Heft 2, 369-78.

        On the relationship of name and "appellative."

322 Fleissner, Robert F.
        "Lear's Learned Name," Names, 22 (1974), 183-4.

        On Lear's name by Shakespeare.

323 Fleming, David A.
        "Names in Allegorical Satire: Barclay's
        'Satyricon'," Names, 16 (1968), 347-56.

324 Flom, Tobias G.
        "Alliteration and Variation in Old Germanic
        Name-Giving," Modern Language Notes, 32
        (1917), 7-17.

        Fluck, Edward J.
        See: 982.

325   Flutre, F.
        "A Review of G. D. West's 'An Index of Proper
        Names...'," Cahiers de Civilisation Médiévale,
        14 (1971), 401-3.

        On names in French Arthurian verse romances.

---, See: 1292.

326   ---, Table des noms propres avec toutes leurs
        variantes, figurant dans les romans de Moyen
        Age écrits en français ou en provençal et
        actuellement publiés ou analysés. Poitiers,
        Centre d'Études Supérieures de Civilisation
        Médiévale, 1962. (Publications de Centre, 2)

        A glossary of names in the chansons de geste.

327   Fonjakova, O. I.
        "Toponimija Nižnego Novgoroda v avtobiografi-
        českich povestjach M. Gor'kogo," Onomastika
        Povolž'ja, 2 (1971), 321-6.

        On the toponym "Nižni Novgorod" in the autho-
        biographical works of Gorkij.

328   Fontes, Henrique da Silva
        Nomes germânicos de pessoas. Florianópolis,
        Faculdade Catarinense de Filosofia, 1959.
        (Série filologica, no. 1)

        On German personal names.

329   Foraboschi, Daniele
        Onomasticon alterum papyrologicum. Supplemento
        al 'Namenbuch' di F. Preisigke. Milano, Ist.
        Editoriale Cisalpino, 1967.

        A supplement to F. Preisigke's "Namenbuch."
        On personal names in Greek manuscrips (papyri).
        Introduction in English, French, Italian and
        German.

330   Forester, C. S.
        "On Names of His Characters, An Interview,"
        Names, 1 (1953), 245-51.

331   Förstemann, Ernst Wilhelm
          Altdeutsches Namenbuch. 2 vols. Bonn,
          Hanstein, 1901. Reprint: München, Fink,
          1966-7.

          See also his "Ergänzungsband." Ed. by Henning
          Kaufmann. München, Fink, 1968.

          On Old German personal names.

332   Forster, John
          The Life of Charles Dickens. 3 vols. London,
          Chapman, 1872-4.

          On names, see Vol. 3, pp. 262-5.

333   Foster, Idris L.
          "The Irish Influence on Some Welsh Personal
          Names," in Essays and Studies Presented to
          Professor Eoin MacNeill .... Ed. by John Ryan,
          Dublin, The Sign of the Three Candles, 1940.

          On names in the romance of Kulhwoh ao Olwen.
          See pp. 28-86.

334   Foucault, Michel
          Les mots et les choses. Paris, Gallimard,
          1966.

          On names, general. See also the English
          edition: The Order of Things; an Archaelogy
          of the Human Sciences. New York, Pantheon,
          1971. (World of Man)

335   Fourquet, Jean
          Le noms propres du Parzival. Mélanges de
          philologie romane et de littérature médiévale.
          Paris, Hoepffner, 1949. (Publications de la
          Faculté des Lettres de l'Université de Stras-
          bourg, 113)

          See pp. 244-60 on names in "Parzival."

336   Fowler, W. W.
          "The Dickens Names," The Galaxy, 8 (September
          1869), 420-2.

Dear Prof. Bryant:

Just a token of appreciation for your help & kindness.

With best wishes,
Elizabeth M. Rajec

Fraenkel, Ernst
    See: 1119.

337 Francis, W. A.
        "Motif of Names in Bourjaily's 'The Hound
        of Earth'," Critique, 17 (1976), 64-72.

        Mostly on geographical names.

338 Francke, W.
        "Another Derivation of Teufelsdröckh,"
        Notes and Queries, 21 (1974), 339-40.

        On a name by Carlyle.

339 Frank, Irmgard
        "A Review of Algeo's 'On Defining the Proper
        Name'," Beiträge zur Namenforschung, 12
        (1977), 107.

    ---, See: 14.

340 Frank, Roberta
        "Some Uses of Paranomasia in Old English
        Scriptural Verse," Speculum, 47 (1972),
        207-26.

341 Franklin, Julian
        A Dictionary of Nicknames. London, Hamilton,
        1962.

342 Freeman, John William
        Discovering Surnames: Their Origins and
        Meanings. Tring, Shire, 1968. (Discovering
        Guides)

        On names, general.

    ---, See: 793.

343 Freeman, Thomas
        "Myths and Mystification: Names in the
        Writings of Hans Henny Jahnn," Literary
        Onomastics Studies, 3 (1976), 33-55.

344 Frege, J. G.
        "Über Sinn und Bedeutung," Zeitschrift
        für Philosophie und philosophische Kritik,
        100 (1892), 1-50.

        Refers also to names.

345 Freie, Magrita Jantina
        Die Einverleibung der fremden Personennamen
        durch die mittelhochdeutsche höfische Epik.
        Amsterdam, Freie, 1933.

        A Proefschrift. On foreign names in Middle
        High German romance.

346 French, George Russell
        Shakespeareana Genealogia. Part I. Identi-
        fication of the dramatis personae in Shake-
        speare's historical plays: from K. John to
        K. Henry VIII. Notes on characters in Macbeth
        and Hamlet. Persons and places belonging to
        Warwickshire, alluded to in several plays.
        Part II. The Shakespeare and Arden families,
        and their connections: with table of descent.
        London, Macmillan, 1869.

        On names, see pp. 347-50, and 529-34.

347 Freud, Sigmund
        Gesammelte Werke. 17 vols. London, Imago,
        1940-52.

        See Vol. 4, pp. 5-10 on the forgetting of
        first and proper names ("Das Vergessen von
        Eigennamen"). See also other editions.

348 Frings, Theodor
       "Rothari - Rogar - Rothere," <u>Pauls und</u>
       <u>Brunes Beiträge zur Geschichte der deutschen</u>
       <u>Sprache und Literatur</u>, 67 (1945), 368-70.

       On the variations of the above names.

     Fromm, Hans
       See: 454.

     Frushell, R. C.
       See: 56.

349 Funcke, Eberhard W.
       "Die Namen im Märchen," <u>Acta Germanica</u>, 8
       (1973; 1976), 19-42.

       On names in fairy tales.

350 Funke, O.
       "Zur Definition des Begriffes 'Eigenname',"
       in <u>Probleme der englischen Sprache und</u>
       <u>Kultur.</u> Festschrift Johannes Hoops zum 60.
       Geburtstag überreicht von Freunden und
       Kollegen. Heidelberg, Winter, 1925.
       (Germanische Bibliothek. Untersuchungen und
       Texte, Bd. 20)

       See pp. 72-9 on the definition of the proper
       name.

351   Gaffney, W. G.
        "Mark Twain's 'Duke' and 'Dauphin'," <u>Names</u>,
        14 (1966), 175-8.

352   Gaiser, Konrad
        <u>Name und Sache in Platons Kratylos</u>. Heidel-
        berg, Winter, 1974. (Abhandlungen der
        Heidelberger Akademie der Wissenschaften,
        Philosophisch-historische Klasse, Jahrgang
        1974, Abhandlung 3)

        On names and things in Plato's "Kratylos."

353   Gale, Robert L.
        "Manuel Lujon. Another Name by Willa Cather,"
        <u>Names</u>, 11 (1963), 210-1.

354   ---, "Names in James," <u>Names</u>, 14 (1966), 83-108.

        On names by H. James.

355   Gard, René Coulet du
        "About Some Characters of Rabelais. Reality?
        Mystification?" <u>Literary Onomastics Studies</u>,
        2 (1975), 134-40.

356   ---, "Victor Hugo's 'Cromwell'," <u>Literary Onomas-
        tics Studies</u>, 3 (1975), 94-101.

357   Gardiner, Alan Henderson
        <u>Ancient Egyptian Onomastica</u>. 3 vols. London,
        Oxford, 1947.

358   ---, <u>On Proper Names</u>. Paris, Ginneken, 1937.
        (Mélanges de linguistique)

359   -—, <u>The Theory of Proper Names. A Controversial
        Essay</u>. 2nd ed. London, Oxford, 1954.

360   Gargano, J. W.
        "Poe's Morella: A Note on Her Name,"
        <u>American Literature</u>, 47 (1975), 259-64.

361　Gaster, Theodor H.
　　　　　"Names and Nicknames," in his The Holy and
　　　　　the Profane. Evolution of Jewish Folkways.
　　　　　New York, Sloane, 1955.

　　　　　See pp. 33-8.

362　Gāters, A.
　　　　　"Mūsu rokās ieverojams romāns Anšlavs Eglitis.
　　　　　Es nepievienojos, Grāmatu Draugs, 1971,"
　　　　　Latvija, (Eutin), 31/1517, 2.

　　　　　On name symbolism in the works of Anšlavs
　　　　　Eglitis.

363　---, "Die Personennamen in den lettischen Volks-
　　　　　märchen," in Donum Blaticum. To Prof.
　　　　　Christian S. Stang on the occassion of his
　　　　　seventieth birthday 15 March 1970. Ed. by
　　　　　Velta Rūke-Dravina. Stockholm, 1970.

　　　　　On names in Lettish fairy tales, see pp.
　　　　　130-41.

364　---, Raina un Aspazijas velni - Raina un Aspazijas
　　　　　Gadagramata (1970). Vasteras, 1969.

　　　　　See pp. 57-84 on names of devils and witches
　　　　　in Lettish fairy tales and in the plays of
　　　　　Aspazija and Janis Rainis.

365　Gates, Arthur Mathews
　　　　　The Form and Use of the Proper Name in Latin
　　　　　Literature. Johns Hopkins University, 1910.

　　　　　A dissertation.

366　Gauger, Hans-Martin
　　　　　Wort und Sprache. Sprachwissenschaftliche
　　　　　Grundfragen. Tübingen, Niemeyer, 1970.
　　　　　(Konzepte der Sprache und Literaturwissenschaft,
　　　　　3)

　　　　　On words and language; on names, see pp. 45-64.

367 Gawor, Stanislaw
"O funkcjach nazw osobowych i miejscowych w
twórczocci Ignacego Krasickiego," Onomastica
(Wroclaw), 10 (1965), 204-23.

On names by I. Krasicki.

368 Georgiev, Vladimir I.
"Die Herkunft der etruskischen mythologischen
Namen," Beiträge zur Namenforschung, 8 (1973),
139-48.

On the origin of Etruscan mythological names.

369 Gerber, Richard
"Die Magie der Namen bei Henry James,"
Anglia. Zeitschrift für englische Philologie,
81 (1963), 175-97.

On the magic of names by H. James.

370 ---, "Vom Geheimnis der Namen. Eine onomastische
Studie über Lessings dramatisches Werk,"
Neue Rundschau, 76 (1965), 573-86.

On names by Keller.

371 ---, "Wege zu Gottfried Kellers letztem Namen.
Ein Versuch über dichterische Onomastik,"
Beiträge zur Namenforschung, 15 (1964), 308-30.

On names by Lessing.

372 ---, "Zur Namengebung bei Defoe," in Festschrift
für Walter Hübner. Hrsg. von Dieter Riesner
und Helmut Gneuss. Berlin, Schmidt, 1964.

On names by Defoe, see pp. 227-33.

373 Gerhardt, Dietrich
"Über die Stellung der Namen im lexikalischen
System," Beiträge zur Namenforschung, 1
(1949-50), 1-24.

On names in the lexicographical system.

374 ---, "Zur Theorie der Eigennamen," Beiträge zur
Namenforschung, 12 (1977), 398-418.

On the theory of proper names.

375 Gerhardt, Elisabetha
Onomasticon Ciceronianum et fastorum ....
Patavii, Livianis, 1968. (Scriptorum
Romanorum quae extant omnia 116-20)

On Cicero's names.

376 Gero, Stephen
"A Note on the Name of Wulfila in Greek and
Syriac," Beiträge zur Namenforschung, 12
(1977), 154-6.

377 Gerus-Tarnavets'ka, Iraida
"Literary Onomastics," Names, 16 (1968),
312-24.

378 ---, "Names of Mountains in Poetry," in Proceed-
ings of the 9th International Congress of
Onomastic Sciences. University College,
London, July 3-8, 1966. Louvain, International Centre of Onomastics, 1969.

See pp. 1-10, and 149-59.

379 ---, Nazovnytstvo v poetyčnomu tvori. (Die Namen
im Kunstwerk des Dichters. Names in Poetry.)
München, Winnipeg, 1966.

Mainly on Ukrainian literary onomastics.

380 ---, "Onomastic Aspects of Ostromir Gospel," in
Festschrift V. Taszycki. Wroclaw, 1968.

See pp. 91-6 on Bible. New Testament Gospels;
Church Slavic.

381 Gilbert, Allan H.
"The Italian Names in 'Every Man Out of His
Humour'," Studies in Philology, 44 (1947),
195-208.

On names by B. Jonson.

382 Gill, Donald A.
"Charactonyms in Gay's 'The Beggar's Opera',"
in Of Edsels and Marauders. Ed. by F. Tarpley
and A. Moseley. Commerce, Texas, Names Institute Press, 1971. (South Central Names Institute Publication No. 1)

See pp. 107-13.

383 Gillespie, George T.
A Catalogue of Persons Named in Germanic
Heroic Literature (700-1600); Including Named
Animals and Objects and Ethnic Names. Oxford,
Clarendon, 1973.

Based on the author's thesis, University of
London.

384 Gilmore, J. H.
"How Shall we Spell Sh-K-SP-R-'S Name?"
Scribner's Monthly, 12 (May 1876), 13-5.

385 Giordano, Charles B.
"On the Significance of Names in Hofmannsthal's
'Rosenkavalier'," The German Quarterly, 36
(1963), 258-68.

386 Gipper, Helmut
Bausteine zur Sprachinhaltsforschung. Neuere
Sprachinhaltsforschungen im Austausch mit
Geistes- und Naturwissenschaft. 2. Aufl.
Düsseldorf, Pedagogischer Verlag, 1969.

On names, theoretical.

387 Glück, C. W.
Die bei Caius Julius Caesar vorkommenden
keltischen Namen in ihrer Echtheit festgestellt
und erläutert. München, Literarisch-artistische
Anstalt, 1857.

On Celtic names by Caesar.

Gneuss, Helmut
See: 372.

388 Golden, John
"An Onomastic Allusion in Caedmon's Hymn,"
Neuphilologische Mitteilungen, 70 (1969),
627-9.

389 Goldfarb, Clare R.
"Names in 'The Bostonians'," Iowa English
Yearbook, 13 (1968), 18-23.

On names by H. James.

390 Goldman, J.
"Insight into Milton's Abdiel," Philological
Quarterly, 49 (1970), 249-54.

391 ---, "Name and Function of Harapha in Milton's
Samson Agonistes," English Languate Notes,
12 (1974), 84-91.

392 Goldsmith, Arnold L.
"The Peotry of Names in 'The Spoils of
Poynton'," Names, 14 (1966), 134-42.

On names by H. James.

393 Golius, Theophilus
Onomasticon Latinogermanicum. Cum prefatione
Johannis Sturnii. Strassburg, 1579. Reprint:
New York, Olms, 1972. (Documenta linguistica:
Reihe 1. Wörterbücher des 15. und 16.
Jahrhunderts)

A Latin Germanic onomasticon.

394   Gollas, M.
      "Etymologia Homerova imienia Odyseusza i
      sprawa jej przekladu," Rozprawy Komisji
      Jazykowej Lódzkiego Towarzystwa Naukowego,
      8 (1962), 55-61.

      On names by Homer.

395   Gómez de Silva, Guido
      "The Linguistics of Personal Names. Methodo-
      logy of Their Study and Sample Results,"
      Onoma, 17 (1972-3), 92-136.

396   Gonzáles, Alfonso
      "Onomastics and Creativity in 'Doña Bárbara
      y Pedro Páramo'," Names, 21 (1973), 40-5.

      On names by Rómulo Gallegos and Juan Rulfo.

397   Goode, Gaylia M.
      The Appropriate Name in Petronius. Univer-
      sity of Illinois at Urbana Champaign, 1939.

      A dissertation.

398   Gordon, Elizabeth Hope
      The Naming of Characters in the Works of
      Charles Dickens. Lincoln, 1917. (University
      of Nebraska Studies in Language, Literature
      and Criticism, 1)

399   Gorskij, Konrad
      "Onomastyka Mickiewica," Onomastica, 6 (1960),
      1-47.

      On names by Mickiewicz.

400   Gottlieb, Eugene
      A Systematic Tabulation of Indo-European
      Animal Names with Special Reference to Their
      Etymology and Semasiology. Philadelphia,
      University of Pennsylvania, 1931. (Language
      Dissertations, No. 8)

      Published subsequently also as a thesis.

401   Gottschald, Max
      Deutsche Namenkunde. Unsere Familiennamen
      nach ihrer Entstehung und Bedeutung. 4. Aufl.
      Mit einem Nachwort und einer Bibliographie.
      Nachtr. von Rudolf Schützeichel. Berlin, de
      Gruyter, 1971.

      On German onomastics - the origin and the
      meaning of our family names. On literary
      onomastics, see pp. 71-3.

402   ---, Die deutschen Personennamen. Berlin, de
      Gruyter, 1955. (Sammlung Goschen, Bd. 422)

      On German personal names.

      Graaff, Robert V., De
      See: DeGraaff, Robert V.

403   Gramenz, Friedrich T., and Valentin Kiparsky
      Englische und pseudoenglische Namen bei
      russischen Schriftstellern. Wiesbaden,
      Harrassowitz, 1961. (Veröffentlichungen der
      Abteilung für Slavische Sprachen und Literatur
      der Osteuropäischen Institute, 25)

      On Russian literary onomastics.

404   Granger, Byrd
      "The Myth of the Cowboy and Westerner: Names
      in Some Works by Zane Grey," Literary Onomas-
      tics Studies, 3 (1976), 120-44.

405   Graur, Alexandru
      Nume de persoane. Bucaresti, Ed. Stiintifica,
      1965.

      On Rumanian personal names, general.

406   Gray, Dorothea H. Forbes
      "Mycenaen Names in Homer," Journal of Hellenic
      Studies, 78 (1958), 43-8.

407 Gray, George Buchanan
       "Children Names After Ancestors in the Aramaic
       Papyri from Elephantine and Assuan ...,"
       Studien zur semitischen Philosophie und Religion
       (1914), 161-76.

408 ---, Studies in Hebrew Proper Names. London,
       Black, 1896.

409 Gray, Ronald
       "But Kafka Wrote in German," The Cambridge
       Quarterly, 7 (1977), 205-16.

       See particularly pp. 206-7 on names.

410 Green, Carleton
       The Place-Names in the "Historia Ecclesias-
       tica" of Bede. Harvard University, 1936.

       A dissertation.

411 Green, E., and R. M. Green
       "Keats's Use of Names in Endymion and in
       the Odes," Studies in Romanticism, 16
       (1977), 15-34.

412 Green, Lola Beth
       "Names in the Bible Belt: A Study from
       Faulkner's 'Go Down Moses'," in They Had to
       Call It Something. Ed. by F. Tarpley.
       Commerce, Texas, Names Institute Press, 1974.
       (South Central Names Institute Publication
       No. 3)

       See pp. 117-20.

     Green, R. M.
       See: 411.

413 Green, William
       "Humours Characters and Attributive Names
       in Shakespeare's Plays," Names, 20 (1972),
       157-65.

414 Greenwood, Granville George
      Is There a Shakespeare Problem? With a
      Reply to J. M. Robertson and A. Lang.
      London, Lane, 1916.

      On Shakespeare's name, see pp. 335-49.

415 Griffin, Barbara Jean
      Naming as a Literary Device in the Novels of
      Charles Dickens. Indiana University, 1970.

      A dissertation.

416 Grimes, Margaret
      "Kafka's Use of Cue-Names; Its Importance
      for an Interpretation of 'The Castle',"
      The Centennial Review, 18 (1974), 221-30.

417 Grimme, Fritz
      "Anklänge an das deutsche Volksepos in
      Ortsnamen," Germania, 32 (1887), 65-72.

      On German toponyma in heroic poetry.

418 Gros, Louis Dolores Kay
      Shakespeare by Many Other Names: Modern
      Dramatic Adaptations. The University of
      Wisconsin, 1968.

      A dissertation.

419 Grünberg, P.
      "Namengebung im Kirschspiel," Die Heimat,
      69 (1962), 241.

      On name giving in church plays.

420 Grycjutenko, I. J.
      "Estetyčna funkcija antroponimiv v
      ukrajinskij hudožnij prozi 50-70 rokiv
      XIX st.'" Visnyk L'vivskogo deržavnogo
      universytetu. Serija filologična, 6 (1969).

      On esthetic functions of personal names in
      Ukrainian literary prose of the 1850s and
      1860s. See pp. 49-50.

421 Grygoruk, O. P.
      "Antroponimija hudožnik tvoriv L. Martovyča,"
      Respublikanska Onomastyčna Konferencija
      Kyjiv, 4 (1969), 131-4.

      On personal names in the works of L. Martovych.'

422 Grzeszczuk, S.
      "Nazewnictwo sowizdraskie," Onomastica,
      16 (1971), 274-8.

      On punning with names.

      Gudeman, Alfred
          See: 24.

      Guin, Ursula K. le
          See: Le Guin, Ursula K.

423 Guirec, J.
      "Histoire d'un nom," Cahiers Haut-marnais,
      96 (1969), 1-5.

      On pseudonyms.

424 Gustavs, Arnold
      Namenreihen aus den Kerkuk-Tafeln. Studien
      zum Bau der Mitanni-Namen, 1937. Reprint:
      Osnabrück, Zeller, 1972. (Mitteilungen der
      altorientalischen Gesellschaft, Bd. 10, H. 3)

      On Mitanni names of the Kerkuk tablets.

425 Gutenbrunner, Siegfried
      "Rin skal ráda. Namenkundliches zur Dichtung
      vom Nibelungenhort," Rheinische Vierteljahrs-
      blätter, 20 (1955), 30-53.

      On the name of Nibelungenhort.

426 ---, "Über die Quellen der Erexsaga. Ein namen-
kundlicher Beitrag zu den Erec-Problemen,:
<u>Archiv für das Studium der neueren Sprachen
und Literaturen</u>, 105 (1954), 1-20.

On sources and names in the Erex Saga.

427 ---, "Über einige Namen in der Nibelungendichtung,"
<u>Zeitschrift für deutsches Altertum und
deutscher Literatur</u>, 85 (1954-5), 44-64.

On names in the Nibelungen.

428 ---, <u>Von Hildebrand und Hadubrand. Lied-Saga-
Mythos</u>. Mit einem Anklang über "Anwendung
graphischer Konstruktion auf die Litera-
turgeschichte." 1976. (Germanische Bibliothek 3. Untersuchungen und Einzeldarstellungen)

On Hildebrand und Hadubrand.

---, See: 1255.

429 Haag, Herbert
      Bibel Lexikon. 2. neubearb. und verm.
      Auflage. Zürich, Benziger, 1968.

      A lexicon of the Bible, passim on names.

Haas, Alois M.
      See: 1056.

Haas, Herta
      See: 637.

430 Hagström, St.
      "Zur Inversion in deutschen Satzwörtern,"
      Uppsala Universitets Arsskrift, 8 (1952).

      On sentence words; also on descriptive
      names.

431 Hales, John W.
      "The Name Shakespeare," _The Athenaeum_,
      Pt. II (August 15, 1903), 230-2.

432 Halfmann, Ulrich
      "Zur Symbolik der Personennamen in den
      Dramen O'Neills," _Herrig's Archiv für das_
      Studium der neueren Sprachen, 121 (1969),
      38-45.

      On symbolic names by O'Neill.

      ---, See: 1101.

433 Halliwell-Phillipps, James Orchard
      New Lamps or Old? A Few Additional Words
      on the Momentous Question Respecting the
      E and A in the Name of Our National Dramatist.
      Brighton, Fleet, 1880.

      On the spelling of Shakespeare's name.

434 ---, <u>Which Shall It Be? New Lamps or Old?</u>
     <u>Shaxpere or Shakespeare?</u> Brighton, Fleet,
     1879.

435 Halsey, William D.
         See: <u>The New Century Cyclopedia of Names</u>.

         On names, general.

436 Hamer, D.
         "Was William Shakespeare William Shakespeare?"
         <u>The Review of English Studies</u>, 21 (1970),
         41-8.

     Hammond, William K.
         See: 1010.

     Hamst, Olphar (pseud.)
         See: 1213.

437 Haney, John Louis
         <u>The Name of William Shakespeare. A Study</u>
         <u>in Orthography</u>. Philadelphia, Egerton,
         1906.

438 Hanning, Robert W.
         "Uses of Names in Medieval Literature,"
         <u>Names</u>, 16 (1968), 325-38.

439 Harder, Kelsie B.
         "A Review of B. R. Pollin's 'Poe: Creator
         of Words'," <u>Names</u>, 24 (1976), 212-4.

     ---, See: 918.

440 ---, "A Review of J. K. Stark's 'Personal Names
         in Palmyrene Inscriptions'," <u>Names</u>, 24
         (1976), 223-4.

     ---, See: 1138.

441 ---, "A Review of 'Literary Onomastics Studies,
       v. 2-3'," Names, 25 (1977), 102-4.

     ---, See: 18.

442 ---, "Charactonyms in Faulkner's Novels,"
       Bucknell Review, 8 (1959), 189-201.

443 ---, "Charles Dickens Names His Characters,"
       Names, 7 (1959), 35-42.

444 ---, "The Names of Thomas Dekker's Devils,"
       Names, 3 (1955), 210-8.

445 Hardie, Colin
       "Inferno XV, 9: Anzi che Chiarentana il
       caldo senta," Modern Language Notes, 79
       (1964), 47-57.

       On names by Dante.

446 Harding, Gerald Lankester
       An Index and Concordance of Pre-Islamic
       Arabian Names and Inscriptions. Toronto,
       University of Toronto Press, 1971.

       On Arabic names.

     Harms, Wolfgang
       See: 454.

447 Harrison, E. L.
       "A Reply With Rejoinder to Horsfall's
       Corythus," Classical Quarterly, 26 (1976),
       293-7.

     ---, See: 513.

448 Harrison, Henry
      Surnames of the United Kingdom: A Concise
      Etymological Dictionary. Assisted by Gyda
      Pulling. London, Eaton, 1912-8.

      On English personal names.

449 Hartig, Joachim
      Die münsterländischen Rufnamen im späten
      Mittelalter. Köln, Böhlau, 1967.
      (Niederdeutsche Studien, Bd. 14)

      On medieval names, see p. 27, passim.
      See also dissertation: Münster, 1965.

450 Hartmann, Peter
      Das Wort als Name. Struktur, Konstitution
      und Leistung der benennenden Bestimmung.
      Köln, Westdeutscher Verlag, 1958. (Wissen-
      schaftliche Abhandlungen der Arbeitsgemein-
      schaft für Forschung des Landes Nordrhein-
      Westfalen, Bd. 6)

      On the word as name.

451 Harvey, Lawrence E.
      "Intellectualism in Corneille: The Symbolism
      of Proper Names in 'La Suivante'," Symposium,
      13 (1959), 290-3.

452 Hassall, William Owen
      History Through Surnames. Oxford, Perga-
      mon, 1967.

    Hassett, Roland Blenner
      See: Blenner-Hassett, Roland

453 Hastings, James
      A Dictionary of the Bible. Dealing with
      its language, literature, and contents,
      including the Biblical theology. 5 vols.
      New York, Scribner's 1898-23.

      On Biblical names, passim.

454 Haubrichs, Wolfgang
        "Veriloquium nominis. Zur Namensexegese
        im frühen Mittelalter. Nebst einer Hypothese
        über die Identität des 'Heliand'—Autors,"
        in Verbum et signum. Hrsg. von Hans Fromm,
        Wolfgang Harms, Uwe Ruberg. 2 vols.
        München, Fink, 1975.

        On medieval names and on the identity of the
        author of the "Heliand," see pp. 231-66.

    Hauck, Karl
        See: 497.

455 Hausmanis, V.
        Raina dailrades process. Riga, Izdevnieciba
        Zinātne, 1971.

        See pp. 291-7 on personal names in the
        dramas of Janis Rainis.

456 ---, "Raina tragēdija 'Ilja Muromietis' tapšanas
        gaita," Karogs (Riga), 8 (1969), 133-40.

        On personal names in the drama "Ilja
        Muromietis" by Janis Rainis.

457 Heckscher, William S.
        "Is Grete's Name Really So Bad?" The
        Manitoba Arts Review, 4 (Spring 1945),
        26-32.

        On the name "Grete" in literature.

458 Heeroma, Klaas
        "Grimhild und Kriemhilt," Jahrbuch des
        Vereins für niederdeutsche Sprachfor-
        schung, 83 (1960), 17-21.

        On the above names in German heroic liter-
        ature.

459   ---, "De localisering van de tweede Reinaert,"
      Tijdschrift voor Nederlandsche Taal- en
      Letterkunde, 86/3 (1970), 161-93.

      On "Zuidholland" as a toponym of the above
      work.

460   Heimeran, Ernst
      Namensbüchlein. München, Heimeran, 1936.

      On personal names.

461   ---, Vornamenbuch. Geschichte und Deutung.
      Mit Namenstagen, Namenspatronen und Namens-
      vorbildern. Erw. und bearb. von Hellmut
      Rosenfeld. Müchen, Heimeran, 1968.

      On the history and meaning of first names.

462   Heinrich, P.
      Die Namen der Hamlettragödie. Leipzig,
      Faberland, 1904.

      On names by Shakespeare.

463   Heinrichs, Heinrich Matthias
      "Sivrit - Gernot - Kriemhilt," Zeitschrift
      für deutsches Altertum und deutsche Liter-
      tur, 86 (1955-6), 279-89.

      On the above names in the Nibelungen.

464   Heintze, Albert
      Die deutschen Familiennamen. Geschichtlich,
      geographisch, sprachlich. Hrsg. von Paul
      Cascorbi. 7. verb. Aufl. Halle, Buchhand-
      lung des Waisenhauses, 1933.

      On German family names.

465 Heldmann, Karl
Die Rolandsbilder Deutschlands in dreihundert-
jähriger Forschung und nach den Quellen.
Halle, Niemeyer, 1904. (Beiträge zur
Geschichte der mittelalterlichen Spiele und
Fälschungen)

On names in Roland.

466 Heller, Erich
The Disinherited Mind. Cleveland, World,
1969.

On names by Kafka, see pp. 197-231.

467 Heller, L. G.
"Two Pequot Names in American Literature,"
American Speech, 36 (1961), 54-7.

Heller, Murray
See: 935.

468 Hellfritzsch, Volkmar
"Zum Problem der stilistischen Funktion
von Namen," in Der Name in Sprache und
Gesellschaft, Berlin (Ost-), 1973.
(Beiträge zur Theorie der Onomastik.
Deutsch-slawische Forschungen zur Namenkunde
und Siedlungsgeschichte, Nr. 27)

On the stylistic functions of names.

469 Hellinga, W. G.
"Naamgevingsproblemen in de Reynaert,"
Anthroponymica, 5 (1952), 1-28.

On names in the "Reynard."

470 Hellwig, Hermann
Untersuchungen über die Namen des nord-
humbrischen Liber Vitae I. Berlin, 1888.

On names in the "Liber Vitae I."

Helm, Karl
    See: 881.

471 Henbeck, A.
        "Zu einigen Namen auf den Pylos Tafeln
        1960," <u>Kadomos</u>, 1 (1962), 59-64.

        On names in the Pylos tablets.

472 Hench, Atchenson L.
        "Study of Names: A Bibliography,"
        <u>American Speech</u>, 12 (1937), 307-9.

        On names, general.

473 Henderson, William
        <u>A Dictionary and Concordance of the Names
        of Persons and Places, and of Some of the
        More Remarkable Terms, Which Occur in the
        Scriptures of the Old and New Testaments.</u>
        Edinburgh, Clark, 1869.

474 Henry, F.
        "L'Onomastique des 'Fleurs de mal'," <u>Revue
        Internationale d'Onomastique</u>, 26 (1974),
        293-301.

        On names by Baudelaire.

475 Henshaw, Richard A.
        "Some Puzzling Aspects of the Aetiological
        Narratives in the Book of Genesis," <u>Liter-
        ary Onomastics Studies</u>, 3 (1976), 22-32.

476 Herber, Joseph
        "Die biblischen Eigennamen im Althochdeut-
        schen besonders bei Otfrid von Weissenburg,"
        <u>Archiv für elsässische Kirchengeschichte</u>,
        4 (1929), 115-36.

        On Old High German Biblical names, partic-
        ularly by Otfrid von Weissenburg.

477 Hergemöller, Bernd-Ulrich
     <u>4400 gebräuchliche Vornamen; Herkunft,
     Deutung, Namensfest</u>. 3. Auflage. Münster,
     Regensberg, 1972.

     On the origin and the meaning of first names.

478 Hermand, Jost
     "Peter Spinell," <u>Modern Language Notes</u>, 79
     (1964), 439-47.

     On names in Thomas Mann's "Tristan."

479 Herrle, Theo
     See: <u>Reclams Namenbuch</u>.

---, See: 629, 953.

Herthum, Paul
     See: 1269.

480 Heubeck, A.
     "Bemerkungen zu einigen griechischen
     Personennamen auf den Linear B-Tafeln,"
     <u>Beiträge zur Namenforschung</u>, 8 (1957),
     28-35.

     A commentary to Greek personal names of
     the Linear-B tablets.

481 ---, "Weitere Bemerkungen zu den griechischen
     Personennamen auf Linear B-Tafeln,"
     <u>Beiträge zur Namenforschung</u>, 8 (1957), 268-78.

     Additional comments to Greek personal names
     of the Linear-B tablets.

482 ---, "Zu einigen Namen auf den Pylos-Tafeln 1960,"
     <u>Kadomos</u>, 1 (1962), 59-64.

     On some of the names of the Pylos tablets.

483 Heuer, H.
"A Review of Kökeritz's 'Shakespeare's Names'," Shakespeare Jahrbuch, 96 (1960), 258-9.

---, See: 613.

484 Heylii, G. d'
Dictionnaire des pseudonymes. Nouvelle édition. Genève, Slatkine Reprints, 1971.

A dictionary of pseudonyms.

485 Highet, G.
"What's in a Name?" in his Talents and Geniuses. The Pleasures of Appreciation. New York, Oxford, 1957.

On names by Shakespeare, Dickens, and others. See pp. 231-7.

486 Hill, Thomas D.
"Raguel and Ragnel: Notes on the Literary Genealogy of a Devil," Names, 22 (1974), 145-9.

On the above names in Middle English.

487 ---, "Sapiential Structure and Figural Narrative in the Old English 'Elene'," Traditio, 27 (1971), 159-77.

On names in "Elene."

488 Hilson, J. C., and R. Nicol
"Two Notes on Sir Charles Grandison," Notes and Queries, 22 (1975), 492-3.

489 Hinkle, D. P.
"Onomastics and the 'Book of Good Love'," Names, 16 (1968), 27-42.

On names by the Archpriest of Hita.

490 Hinkulov, L.
          "Psevdonimika, i zavdannja i problemy,"
          Rad. Literaturoznavstvo (Kyjiv), 8 (1971),
          31-42.

          On pseudonyms.

491 Hinton, N. D.
          "Two Names in 'The Reeve's Tale'," Names,
          9 (1961), 117-20.

          On names by Chaucer.

492 Hinz, Evelyn J.
          "Henry James's Names: Tradition, Theory
          and Method," Colby Library Quarterly, 9
          (1972), 557-78.

493 Hinze, Otto
          Studien zu Ben Jonsons Namengebung in seinen
          Dramen. Leipzig, 1919.

          A dissertation on Jonson's names.

494 Hirata, Ryuichi
          L'onomastica falisca e i suoi reapporti con
          la latina e l'utrasca. Firenze, Olschki,
          1967. (Bibliotheca di studi etruschi, 3)

          On Faliscan names.

495 Hirzel, Rudolf
          "Der Name: Ein Beitrag zu seiner Geschichte
          im Altertum und besonders bei den Griechen,"
          Sächsische Akademie der Wissenschaften.
          Philologisch-historische Klasse, Abhandlungen,
          36 (1918), 1-108.

          On the history of the name, particularly by
          the Greeks. See also the reprint: Amsterdam,
          Hakkert, 1962.

496 Hodge, James L.
          "'Rhodope': By Any Other Name?" Modern
          Language Notes, 79 (1964), 435-9.

          On names by Friedrich Hebbel.

Hoffmann, Ernst
    See: 504.

Hoffmann, Werner
    See: 1274.

497 Höfler, Otto
    "Die Anonymität des Nibelungenliedes," in
    Zur germanisch-deutschen Heldensage. Sechzehn
    Aufsätze zum neuen Forschungsstand. Hrsg. von
    Karl Hauck. Darmstadt, Wissenschaftliche
    Buchgesellschaft, 1961. (Wege der Forschung,
    Bd. 14)

    On names in the Nibelungen. See pp. 330-92.

498 ---, Siegfried, Arminius und die Symbolik. Mit
    einem historischen Anhang über die Varus-
    schlacht. Heidelberg, Winter, 1961.

    On names in the Nibelungen, passim on names.

499 Holden, Hubert A.
    Onomasticon Aristophaneum sive index nominum
    quae apud Aristophaneum leguntur. Cambridge,
    1902. Reprint: New York, Olms, 1970.

    An onomasticon of Aristophanes.

500 Hollander, Lee M.
    "Hagen der Tronegaere," Neophilologus,
    53 (1969), 398-402.

    On names in German heroic literature.

501 Hollis, Carrol C.
    "Names in 'Leaves of Grass'," Names, 5
    (1957), 129-56.

    On names by Whitman.

502 Holthausen, Ferdinand
     "Studien zur Thidrekssaga," Beiträge zur
     Geschichte der deutschen Sprache und
     Literatur, 9 (1884), 451-503.

     On names in the Thidreks Saga.

503 ---, Vergleichendes und etymologisches Wörterbuch
     des altwestnordischen, altnorwegischisländischen,
     einschliesslich der Lehn- und Fremdwörter
     sowie der Eigennamen. Göttingen, Vandenhoech,
     1948.

     A comparative and etymological dictionary of
     personal names.

504 Honecker, Martin
     Der Name des Nicolaus von Cues in zeitgenös-
     sischer Etymologie, zugleich ein Beitrag
     zum Problem der Onomastik. Vorgelegt von
     Ernst Hoffmann. Heidelberg, Winter, 1940.
     (Sitzungsberichte der Heidelberger Akademie
     der Wissenschaften. Philologisch-histor-
     ische Klasse, 1939-40)

     On the name of Nicolaus Cusanus.

505 Honl, Ivan
     "Šafárikův výklad názvu Krkonoš a jeho ohlas
     v české literature," Krkonoše-Podkrkonoši
     3 (1967), 233-40.

     On the toponym "Krkonoš" by Šafárik and also
     in Czech literature.

506 ---, "Toponymické etymologie z českého lidového
     podáni," Onomastické Práce (Praha), 2
     (1968), 59-63.

     On toponyma in Czech folklore.

507 Hoops, Johannes
        Shakespeares Name und Herkunft.
        Heidelberg, Winter, 1941. (Sitzungs-
        berichte der Heidelberger Akademie
        der Wissenschaften. Philosophisch-
        historische Klasse, 1940-41)

        See also "Shakespeare's Name and Origin,"
        in _Studies for William A. Read_; ed. by
        Nathaniel M. Caffee and Thomas A. Kirby.
        Freeport, Books for Libraries Press;
        reprint of the 1940 edition.

        ---, See: 350, 681, 972.

508 Horn, Wilhelm
        "Der Name Shakespeare," _Archiv_, 185 (1948),
        26-35.

        On Shakespeare's name.

509 Horne, Charles Ellsworth
        Personal Names in the Sargon Letters.
        University of Chicago, 1907.

        A dissertation.

510 Hornung, Herwig Hans
        See: _Aus dem Namengut Mitteleuropas._

        A collection of essays on Middle European
        names.

511 Hornung, Maria
        See: _Aus dem Namengut Mitteleuropas._

        A collection of essays on Middle European
        names.

512 Horrell, Joyce Tayloe
        "A Shade of a Special Sense: Henry James
        and the Art of Naming," _American Literature_,
        42 (1970), 203-20.

513 Horsfall, N.
         "Corythus: The Return of Aeneas in Virgil
         and His Sources," Journal of Roman Studies,
         63 (1973), 68-79.

     ---, See: 447.

     Houtchens, Carolyn Washburn
         See: 524.

     Houtchens, Lawrence Huston
         See: 524.

514 Howe, Nicholas Phillies
         "Chaucer's Use of Trumpyngtoun in 'The
         Reeve's Tale'," Names, 24 (1976), 324.

515 Howell, Elmo
         "Eudora Welty and the Poetry of Names: A
         Note on Delta Wedding," in Love and Wrest-
         ling, Butch, and O. K. Ed. by Fred Tarpley.
         Commerce, Texas, Names Institute Publica-
         tion No. 2)

516 ---, "A Name for Faulkner's City," Names, 16
         (1968), 415-21.

     Hübner, Walter
         See: 372.

517 Hubschmid, Johannes
         Bibliographica onomastica Helvetica.
         Bernae, Bibliotheca Nationalis, 1954.

         A bibliography on Swiss names. See also
         Onoma, 3 (1952), 1-52.

518 Huff, Lloyd D.
         Place-Names in Chaucer. Indiana Univer-
         sity, 1950.

         A dissertation.

519 Hughes, Charles James Pennethorne
          How You Got Your Name: The Origin and
          Meaning of Surnames. London, Phoenix
          House, 1959.

          See also the revised edition, 1961.

520 ---, Is Thy Name Wart? The Origins of Some
          Curious and Other Surnames. London,
          Phoenix House, 1965.

521 Hugon, Paul Desdemaines
          "Proper Names," in his Morrow's Word-
          Finder. A living guide to modern usage,
          spelling, synonyms, pronunciation, gram-
          mar, word origin and authorship. New York,
          Morrow, 1927.

          See particularly pp. 212-5.

522 Huisman, J. A.
          "A Review of Falk's 'Das Nibelungenlied
          in seiner Epoche'," Beiträge zur Namen-
          forschung, 12 (1977), 357-8.

     ---, See: 301.

523 Humbach, H.
          "Die geographischen Namen des altis-
          ländischen Humenschlachtliedes," Germania,
          43 (1969), 146-62.

          On geographical names in the above Old
          Icelandic song.

524 Hunt, Leigh
          "Originality of Milton's Harmonious Use of
          Proper Names," in his Literary Criticism,
          ed. by Lawrence Huston Houtchens and Carolyn
          Washburn Houtchens. With an essay in evolu-
          tion by Clarence De Witt Thorpe. New York,
          Columbia University Press, 1956.

          See pp. 230-8.

525 Hunter, Joseph
         New Illustrations of the Life, Studies,
         and Writings of Shakespeare. 2 vols.
         London, Nichols, 1845.

         See Vol. 1, pp. 1-9 on the surname of
         Shakespeare.

526 ---, "On the Orthography of Shakespeare,"
         The Gentleman's Magazine, 167 (April 1840),
         369-74.

527 Husband, M. F. A.
         Dictionary of the Characters in the Waverly
         Novels of Sir Walter Scott. London, Routledge,
         1910.

528 Hutson, Arthur Eugene
         "British Personal Names," in Historia
         Regum Britanniae. Berkeley, California,
         1940. (University of California Publica-
         tions in English, Vol. 5, No. 1)

529 Ingleby, Clement Mansfield
         Shakespeare. The Man and the Book:
         Being a Collection of Occasional
         Papers on the Bard and His Writings.
         London, Trübner, 1877-81.

         On the meaning of the surnames of
         Shakespeare, see Vol. 1, pp. 12-20;
         on the spelling, see Vol. 1, pp. 1-11.

530 Irvine, Theodora Ursula
         How to Pronounce the Names in Shakespeare.
         The pronunciation of the names in the dra-
         matic personae of each of Shakespeare's
         plays, also the pronunciation and expla-
         nation of place names and the names of all
         persons, mythological characters, etc.,
         found in the text. With forewords by
         E. H. Sothern and Thomas W. Churchill and
         with a list of the dramas arranged alpha-
         betically indicating the pronunciation of
         the names of the characters in the plays.
         New York, Hinds, 1919. Reprint: Detroit,
         Gale, 1974.

531 ---, A Pronouncing Dictionary of Shakespearean
         Proper Names. New York, Barnes, 1945.

         Originally published as How to Pronounce
         the Names in Shakespeare.

532 Isani, M. A.
         "Naming of Fedallah in Moby-Dick,"
         American Literature, 40 (1968), 380-5.

         On names by H. Melville.

533 Ising, G.
         "Zu den Tiernamen in den ältesten nieder-
         deutschen Bibeldrucken," Jahrbuch des
         Vereins für niederdeutsche Sprachforschung,
         83 (1960), 41-58.

         On animal names.

Israeli, Isaac D'
    See: D'Israeli, Isaac

534 Istrate, G.
        "Numele de oameni in opera lui Sadoveanu,"
        Cronica, 5/34 (1970), 10.

        On personal names in the works of Sadoveanu.

535 Iventosch, Herman
        "The Elaboration of an Episode from the
        'Quijote' in the 'Dorotea'," Hispanic
        Review, 28 (1960), 215-9.

        On names by Cervantes and Lope de Vega.

536 ---, "Moral-Allegorical Names in Gracián's
        Criticón," Names, 9 (1961), 215-33.

537 ---, "Onomastic Invention in the Buscón,"
        Hispanic Review, 29 (1961), 15-32.

        On names by Quevedo.

538 ---, "Orinda, California: Or, The Literary
        Traces in California Toponymy," Names,
        12 (1964), 103-7.

539 ---, "Spanish Baroque Parody in Mock Titles
        and Fictional Names," Romance Philology,
        15 (1961), 29-39.

540 Jackson, M. P.
"North's Plutarch and the Name Escanes in Shakespeare's Pericles," Notes and Queries, 22 (1975), 173-4.

541 Jaffe, Adrian H.
The Process of Kafka's Trial. East Lansing, Michigan State University Press, 1967.

See pp. 13-7 on "The Function of Names."

542 James, William Powell
"Names in Novels," Blackwood's Edinburgh Magazine, 150 (August 1891), 230-7.

Reprinted also in Littell's Living Age, 190 (September 1891), 813-9, and in The Eclectic Magazine, 117 (October 1891), 456-62.

543 ---, Romantic Professions and Other Papers. London, Mathews, 1894.

See pp. 128-54 for a revised reprint of "Names in Novels."

544 Jampol'skij, Z.
"Ob interpolljacii étnomina tjurki u Pomponija Mely i u Plinija Staršego," Učenye zapiski Azerb. un-ta. Ser. jazyka, literatum, 2 (1970), 10-1.

On names by Pomponius Mela and by Pliny the Elder.

545 Janeway, M.
"Who Is Doris Grumbach? Real Faces Behind the Names in Fiction," Atlantic, 220 (1967), 90-1.

On names in Mary McCarthy's fiction.

546　Janifer, L. M.
　　　　"Game of the Name:　Naming Literary
　　　　Characters," Writer, 89 (1976), 27-8.

　　　　On literary onomastics, general.

547　Janzén, A.
　　　　"Names in the Pidriks Saga," Journal of
　　　　English and Germanic Philology, 61 (1962),
　　　　81-93.

548　Jarvis, S. M.
　　　　Discovering Christian Names.　Aylesbury,
　　　　Shire, 1973.

　　　　Jellinek, Max H.
　　　　See:　1047.

549　Jespersen, Otto
　　　　The Philosophy of Grammar.　London, Allen,
　　　　1924.

　　　　See pp. 65-71 on "Actual Meaning of
　　　　Proper Names."

550　Jocelyn, H. D.
　　　　"Two Plautine Names:　Milphio and Milphi-
　　　　dippa," Classical Review, 21 (1971), 331.

551　Johnson, Rossiter
　　　　A Dictionary of Famous Names in Fiction,
　　　　Drama, Poetry, History and Art.　New York,
　　　　Johnson, 1908.　Reprint:　Detroit, Gale,
　　　　1974.

　　　　Originally published as Vol. 20 of the
　　　　Author's Digest.　The World's Great Stories
　　　　in Brief.　1908.

552　Johnson, V.
　　　　"Ninnius, Vinius, and Onysius:　Suggested
　　　　Emendations of Some Names in Horace,"
　　　　Classical Philology, 35 (1940), 420-2.

Jones, E. E. Duncan
    See: Duncan-Jones, E. E.

553   Jones, John David
    The Hidden and Manifest Divinity: A Study
    and Translation of the "Divine Names" and
    "Mystical Theology" of Pseudo-Dionysius
    Aeropagite. Boston College, 1976.

    A dissertation.

554   Jones, Rowland
    "A Lexicon of Difficult Names and Passages
    in Ancient Authors," in his The Philosophy
    of Words in Two Dialogues Between the
    Author and Crito. Containing, an expla-
    nation, with various specimens, of the
    first language, and thence of all its
    dialects, and the principles of knowledge.
    A lexicon of difficult names and passages
    in the Bible, and ancient authors; and
    a plan for a universal philosophical
    language. London, Hughs, 1769.

    See particularly pp. 46-80.

555   Jones, William M.
    "Name and Symbol in the Prose of Eudora
    Welty," Southern Folklore Quarterly, 22
    (1958), 173-86.

556   Josseé, Roland Dionys
    Nomen et omen. Handbuch der Character-
    und Schicksalsdeutung nach dem System der
    phonetischen Kabbalistik. Freiburg,
    Bauer, 1956.

    On the cabalistics of names.

557   Jünger, Ernst
    Typus, Name, Gestalt. Stuttgart, Klett,
    1963.

    On names, poetical.

558 Kabell, Aa
     "Wieland," Beiträge zur Namenforschung,
     9 (1974), 102-14.

     On "Wieland" in German heroic literature.

559 Kaganoff, Benzion C.
     Dictionary of Jewish Names and Their History.
     New York, Schocken, 1977.

     Kahn, Georg
     See: 1049.

560 Kainz, Friedrich
     "Zur dichterischen Sprachgestaltung,"
     Zeitschrift für Aesthetik und allgemeine
     Kunstwissenschaft, 18 (1925), 195-222.

     On literary onomastics, general.

561 Kajanto, Iiro
     Onomastic Studies in the Early Christian
     Inscriptions of Rome and Carthage. Helsinki,
     1963. (Acta Instituti Romani Finlandiae,
     Vol. 2/1)

562 Kalbow, Werner
     Die germanischen Personennamen des alt-
     französischen Heldenepos und ihre lautliche
     Entwicklung. Halle, Niemeyer, 1913.

     On Germanic personal names in Old French
     heroic epos.

563 Kallsen, T. J.
     "The Undeserved Degeneration of 'Babbitt',"
     Names, 21 (1973), 124-5.

     On names in the works of Sinclair Lewis.

564 Kalverkämper, Hartwig
     <u>Eigennamen und Kontext</u>. University Biele-
     feld, 1976.

     A dissertation on proper names and their
     context.

565 Kamber, G.
     "Allegory of the Names in L'Étranger,"
     <u>Modern Language Quarterly</u>, 22 (1961),
     <u>292-301.</u>

     On names by Albert Camus.

566 Kamerzan, L. D.
     Partikularitécile onomastičij yn
     lukrarja luj Miron Kostin. 'Letopisecul
     Céril Moldovej',' Nauč. konfer. prof. pre-
     podov.... Sekcija <u>obsč. i guman nauk</u>, (1970),
     242-4.

     On literary onomastics in the works of
     M. Costin.

567 Kansaku, K.
     "'Chosen meisho waka yôshô' to Heianchô waka,"
     <u>Kokugo to Kobubungaku/Language and Literature</u>,
     47/4 (1970), 97-113.

     On names in poems of the Heian dynasty.

568 ---, "'Sonenoyoshitada kashû' ni mirareru
     chimeikô," <u>Literary Bulletin, Tokyo Uni-</u>
     <u>versity</u>, 43 (1969), 1-21.

     On toponyma in the above Japanese poems.

569 Karpenko, M. V.
     "O materialach k antroponimičeskomu
     slovarju pisatelja," <u>Respublikanska Onomas-</u>
     <u>tyčna Konferencija Kyjiv</u>, 4 (1969), 154-7.

     On sources of dictionaries on personal names.

570 ---, "Slovoobrazovanije literaturnych antro-
ponimov," Pytannja slovotvoru shidnoslov-
'jans'kych mov. Kyjiv, 1969.

See pp. 137-8 on coinage of literary names.

571 Karsai, G.
"Névtelenség, névrejtés és szerzőnév
középkori kronikáinkban," Századok, 97
(1963), 666-77.

On anonymity, cryptonyms, and authorship
in Hungarian chronicals of the Middle Ages.

572 Kaspers, Wilhelm
"Zu den germanisch flektierten sakralen
Namen auf lateinischen Inschriften,"
Beiträge zur Namenforschung, 8 (1957\,
289-95.

On Germanic sacral names in Latin inscriptions.

573 Kasym, J. F.
"Slovotvorči osoblyvosti prizvyšč u tvorah
ukrajisnkyh radjanskyh şatyrykiv i gumorystiv,
Respublikanska Onomastyčna Konferencija
Kyjiv, 4 (1969), 134-5.

On formation of names in satirical and
humorous Ukrainian literary works.

574 Katagiri, Y.
"Utamakura no naritate," Kokugo to Kokubungaku
Language and Literature, 47/4 (1970), 22-33.

On Japanese poetical toponyma.

575 Katz, Blanche
La Prise d'Orenge. According to Manuscript
A. 1, Bibliothèque Nationale, Française 774.
Including excerpts published for the first
time from Manuscripts B. 1, C. D. and E.,
and with introductory table of assonances,
glossary and table of proper names. Columbia
University, 1948.

A dissertation.

576 Katz, Rosa (Heine)
        Psychologie des Vornamens. Bern, Huber, 1964.
        (Beihefte zur schweizerischen Zeitschrift
        für Psychologie und ihre Anwendungen, Nr. 48)

        On the psychology of first names.

577 Kaufmann, Henning
        Untersuchungen zu altdeutschen Rufnamen.
        München, Fink, 1965. (Grundfragen der
        Namenkunde, Bd. 3)

        A study of Old Germanic names.

     ---, See: 331.

578 Kayser, Christoph H.
        "Some Observations on Thomas Mann's Use
        of Names in 'Buddenbrooks'," Literary
        Onomastics Studies, 2 (1975), 116-33.

579 Kegel, Ernst
        Die Verbreitung der mittelhochdeutschen
        erzählenden Literatur in Mittel- und
        Niederdeutschland. Nachgewiesen auf
        Grund von Personennamen. Halle, Niemeyer,
        1905. (Hermaea, 3); Reprint: Walluf,
        Sändig, 1972.

        On names in Middle High German epic liter-
        ature.

580 Kehler, Harold
        "James's 'The Real Thing'," Explicator,
        25 (1967), 79.

        On the name "Churm."

581 Kehrein, Joseph
       Onomastisches Wörterbuch. Zugleich ein
       Beitrag zu einem auf die Sprache der
       klassischen Schriftsteller gegründeten
       Wörterbuch der neuhochdeutschen Sprache.
       Wiesbaden, 1863. Reprint: Hildesheim,
       1974.

       A dictionary of onomastics.

582 Keil, Karl
       Specimen onomatologi Graeci. Leipzig,
       Fratres Reichenbach, 1840.

       On Greek onomatology.

583 Keiter, Heinrich, and Tony Kellen
       Der Roman. Geschichte, Theorie und
       Technik des Romans und der erzählenden
       Dichtkunst. 3. verb. und verm. Aufl.
       Essen, Freudebeul, 1908.

       On literary onomastics in German novels,
       see pp. 354-62, passim.

     Kellen, Tony
       See: 583.

     Keller, Wolfgang
       See: 681, 972.

584 Kelling, H. D.
       "Some Significant Names in 'Gulliver's
       Travels'," Studies in Philology, 48
       (1951), 761-78.

       On names by J. Swift.

585 Kellman, Steven G.
       "Dropping Names: The Poetics of Titles,"
       Criticism, 17 (1975), 152-67.

       On correlation between title and name of
       characters.

586 Kellogg, Allen B.
        "Nicknames and Nonce-Names in Shakespeare's
        Comedies," Names, 3 (1955), 1-4.

587 ---, "Place Names and Epithets in Homer and
        Shakespeare," Names, 3 (1955), 169-7.

     Kempers, August Johan Bernet
        See: Bernet-Kempers, August Johan

588 Kempf, Gabriele
        Bibliographie zur deutsch-slawischen
        Namenkunde. Giessen, Schmitz, 1976.
        (Osteuropastudien der Hochschulen des
        Landes Hessen, Reihe 2. Marburger
        Abhandlungen zur Geschichte und Kultur
        Osteuropas, Bd. 17)

        A bibliography on German-Slavic
        onomastics.

589 Kennedy, G. W.
        "Naming and Language in 'Our Mutual Friend',"
        Nineteenth Century Fiction, 28 (1973), 165-78.

        On names by Dickens.

590 Key, David Martin
        The Introduction of Characters by Name in
        Greek and Roman Comedy. University of
        Chicago, 1916.

        A dissertation.

591 Keyser, P. de
        "De namen van Reinaert en Isengrim in de
        middeleeuwse fabelliteratur," Spieghel
        Historiael, 3 (1960), 1-12.

        On Reinaert's and Isengrim's names in fabel
        literature.

592 Kime, Wayne R.
        "The Satiric Use of Names in Irving's
        'History of New York'," Names, 16 (1968),
        380-9.

593 King, K. C.
"On the Naming of Places in Heroic
Literature: Some Examples from the
Nibelungenlied," <u>Oxford German Studies</u>,
2 (1967), 13-24.

594 Kinslaw, Dennis Franklin
<u>A Study of the Personal Names in the</u>
<u>Akkadian Texts from Ugarit</u>. Brandeis
University, 1967.

A dissertation.

Kinpel, B. D.
See: 267.

Kiparsky, V.
See: 403.

595 Kipling, Rudyard
<u>Jungle Books</u>. New York, Doubleday, 1937.

On his notes on names.

Kirby, Thomas A.
See: 507.

596 Kirchberger, L.
"Thomas Mann's 'Tristan'," Germanic
Review, 36 (1961). 282-97.

597 Kirdan, B. P.
"Antroponimy v ulrainskich národnych
dumach," Antroponimika (1971, 322-8.

On personal names in Ukranian national tales.

598 Klaiber, Theodor
"Die Namen im Roman," Das Literarische
Echo, 19 (July 1903), 1311-5.

On names in German novels.

599 Klarmann, Johann Ludwig
       Zur Geschichte der deutschen Familien-
       namen. 2nd ed. Lichtenfeld, Schulze,
       1927.

       On the history of German family names.

600 Kleiber, Wolfgang
       "Zur Namenforschung in Wolframs Parzival,"
       Der Deutschunterricht, 14 (1962), 80-90.

       On names in "Parzival."

     ---, See: 1052.

601 Kleinpaul, Rudolf
       Die deutschen Personennamen, ihre
       Entstehung und Bedeutung. Hrsg. von Hans
       Naumann. Berlin, de Gruyter, 1916.
       (Sammlung Göschen, Bd. 422)

       On the origin and the meaning of German
       personal names.

602 Kletschke, Hans
       Die Sprache der Mainzer Kanzlei nach den
       Namen der Fuldaer Urkunden. Halle, Niemeyer,
       1933. (Hermaes, 29)

       On names in the Fulda text. See also
       dissertation: Halle, Wittenberg, 1932.

603 Klimaj, Z.
       "Imiona i przezwiska bohaterów powiesci
       S. Przybyszewskiego," Roczniki Humanistyczny
       KUL, Jezykoznawstwa, 17/4 (1969), 45-58.

       On names in the novels of S. Przybyszewski.

604 Kliman, Bernice W.
       "Names in 'Portnoy's Complaint'," Critique,
       14, No. 3 (1973), 16-24.

       On names by Phillip Roth.

605 Klinck, Roswitha
       Die lateinische Etymologie des Mittelalters.
       München, Fink, 1970.

       On the etymology of Latin names of the
       Middle Ages, see pp. 62-5.

606 Klopsch, P.
       "Anonimität und Selbstbenennung mittellatei-
       nischer Autoren," Mittellateinisches
       Jahrbuch, 4 (1967), 9-25.

       On anonymity and self-naming of Middle
       Latin authors.

607 Knechtel, Lawrence, A.
       Names and Life Roles. United States
       International University, 1973.

       A dissertation.

608 Knight, George Wilson
       The Sovereign Flower. On Shakespeare as
       the Poet. Index by Patricia M. Ball.
       New York, Macmillan, 1958.

       On "What's in a Name," see pp. 170-2.

609 Knobloch, Johann
       "Profanierte Heiligennamen," in Studien
       zur Namenkunde und Sprachgeographie.
       Festschrift für Karl Finsterwalder zum
       70. Geburtstag. Hrsg. von Wolfgang Meid,
       Hermann M. Ölberg, Hans Schmeja. Innsbruck,
       Institut für Vergleichende Sprachwissen-
       schaft der Universität, 1971. (Innsbrucker
       Beiträge zur Kulturwissenschaft, Bd. 16)

       On names of saints, see pp. 401-3.

610 Knorr, Wilhelm
       Die Familiennamen des Fürstentums. 2 vols.
       Lübeck, Entin, 1876-82.

       On German sovereign names.

611 Kohlheim, Volker
       Regensburger Rufnamen des 13. und 14.
       Jahrhunderts. Linguistische und sozioono-
       mastische Untersuchungen zur Struktur und
       Motivik spätmittelalterlicher Anthroponymie.
       Wiesbaden, Steiner, 1977. (Zeitschrift für
       Dialektologie und Linguistik, Supplement,
       19)

       On medieval names from Regensburg.

612 Kökeritz, Helge
       "Punning Names in Shakespeare," Modern
       Language Notes, 65 (1950), 240-3.

613 ---, Shakespeare's Names. A Pronouncing Dic-
       tionary. New Haven, Yale University Press,
       1959. (Yale Shakespeare Supplements)

     ---, See: 483, 732.

614 Kolatch, Alfred J.
       These Are the Names. New York, David, 1948.

       On Jewish and English personal names.

615 Kolb, Herbert
       Munsalvaesche. Studien zum Kyotproblem.
       München, Eidos, 1963.

       A dissertation. Frei University, Berlin.
       See particularly pp. 9-50 on names in
       Wolfram's "Parzifal."

616 ---, "Der Name des 'Helden'. Betrachtungen zur
Geltung und Geschichte eines Wortes," in
Zeiten und Formen in Sprache und Dichtung.
Festschrift für Fritz Tschirch zum 70.
Geburtstag. Hrsg. von Karl-Heinz Schirmer
und Bernhardt Sowinski. Köln, Böhlau,
1972.

On the meaning and the importance of the
word "hero", see pp. 384-406.

617 ---, "Namen und Bezeichnungen der Pferde in
der mittelalterlichen Literatur,"
Beiträge zur Namenforschung, 9 (1974),
151-6.

On names of horses in literature of the
Middle Ages.

Kolberg, Oskar
See: 649.

618 Kolk, Helmich van der
Das Hildebrandlied. Eine forschungs-
geschichtliche Darstellung. Amsterdam,
Scheltema, 1967.

On names in the "Hildenbrandlied," see
pp. 64-99.

619 Kolokolova, L. I.
Onomastika v chudožestvennoj reči A. P.
Čechova. Kiev, 1970.

A dissertation on literary onomastics in
the works of Chekhov.

620 Komolova, T. I.
"Toponim Peterburg-Petrograd v proizvedenijach
V. I. Lenina," Toponimika, 5 (1971), 7-8.

On the above toponym in Lenin's works.

621 Koss, Gerhard
         "Motivationen bei der Wahl von Rufnamen,"
         Beiträge zur Namenforschung, 7 (1972),
         159-75.

         On the motivation of selecting names.

622 Kovalovszky, Miklós
         "Az iró és a nevek," Nyelvtudományi
         Értekezések, 70 (1970), 167-71.

         On Hungarian authors and their names.

623 Krahe, H.
         "Alt-Germanische völker- und namen-
         geschichtliche Untersuchungen,"
         Indogermanische Forschungen, 54 (1936),
         218-23.

         On Old Germanic names.

624 Králik, Dietrich
         "Nibelung: Schilderung und Balmung,"
         Wiener prähistorische Zeitschrift, 19
         (1932), 324-48.

         On names in the Nibelung.

625 Králik, O.
         "K funkci vlastního jmena v tvorbě Petra
         Bezruče," Slavica Pragensia, 4 (1963),
         721-6.

         On the functions of proper names in the
         works of P. Bezruč, the Czech writer.

626 Kramárik, J.
         "Etymologická podáni z cykly chodských
         lidových tradic o Kozinovi a Lomikárovi,"
         Zpravodaj Mistopisné Komise Československé
         Akademie Věd, 12 (1971), 667-77.

         On the above names in Chod (Czech) folklore.

Kranzmayer, Eberhard
See: 33.

627 Kratz, Henry
"Etymology of the Name Hagen in the
Nibelungenlied," Names, 10 (1962),
101-7.

628 ---, "Methodological Critique of W. R. Maurer's
Names from 'The Magic Mountain'," Names,
11 (1963), 20-5.

On names by Thomas Mann.

---, See: 750.

629 Kremer, D.
"A Review of Herrle's 'Reclam Namenbuch',"
Beiträge zur Namenforschung, 12 (1977),
108-9.

---, See: 905.

630 Kriaras, E.
'Noms propres de provenance italienne
dans le 'Théâtre crétois'. Degré d'érudi-
tion des auteurs," Revue des Études Sud-est
Européenes, 7 (1969), 133-41.

On proper names in the Italian "théâtre
crétois."

631 Krien, Reinhard
Namenphysiognomik. Untersuchungen zur
sprachlichen Expressivität am Beispiel
von Personennamen, Apellativen und
Phonemen des Deutschen. Tübingen,
Niemeyer, 1973.

On the physiognomy of German personal
names.

---, See 110.

632 Krištof, S.
"Osobné mená v novelách Boženy Slánčikovej-
Timravy," Zpravodaj Mistopisné Komise
Československé Akademie Věd, 10 (1969),
713-9.

On personal names in the novels of B.
Slánčiková-Timrava.

633 Krockow, Peter von
Namen und Titel. Vornamen, Familiennamen,
Adels- und Diensttitel nach Ursprung und
Sinn erklärt. Frankfurt, Höchst, 1968.

On German first, family, and nobility
names as well as on titles.

634 Krogmann, Willy
"Manesse," Beiträge zur Namenforschung,
9 (1958), 108-10.

On the above name in German heroic
literature.

635 ---, "Der Name Goethe," Muttersprache, 1
(1950), 30.

On Goethe's name.

636 ---, "Die Nibelungen. Ein namenkundliches
Problem der germanischen Heldensage,"
6. Internationaler Kongress für Namenforschung, 1958.

On a problem of onomastics in the
"Nibelungen." See also Studia Onomastica
Monacensia, 4 (1961), 474-83.

637 ---, and Ulrich Pretzel
Bibliographie zum Nibelungenlied und zur
Klage. 4. ed. Hrsg. von Herta Haas and
Wolfgang Bachofer, 1966. (Bibliographien
zur deutschen Literatur des Mittelalters,
Heft 1)

A bibliography on the "Nibelungenlied" and
the "Klage," passim on names.

638 Kromp, Justina
       Die Personennamen der mittelhochdeutschen
       Heldenepen in den Urkunden vor deren
       Entstehungszeit. Wien, 1942.

       A dissertation on Middle High German
       personal names in heroic literature.

639 Kronik, John W.
       "The Function of Names in the Stories of
       Alas," Modern Language Notes, 80 (1965),
       260-5.

       On names in the stories of L. Alas.

640 Krueger, John R.
       "Names and Nomenclature in Science-Fiction,"
       Names, 14 (1966), 203-14.

641 Krusche, Dietrich
       Kafka und Kafka-Deutung. Die problematisierte
       Interaktion. München, Fink, 1974. (Kritische
       Information, Bd. 5)

       On names by Kafka, see pp. 69-70.

642 Kruse, H. H.
       "A Reply to A. R. Tamke's Study on Gatsby,"
       Modern Fiction Studies, 15 (1969-70), 539-41.

       On the above name by F. Scott Fitzgerald.

     ---, See: 1191.

643 Kubinyi, L.
       "Miért 'Bor' a neve annak a vitéznek?"
       Magyar Nyelv, 59 (1963), 350-1.

       On above mentioned hero's name in the ballad
       of János Arany, the Hungarian poet.

644   Kudlaty, John Michael
        The Stylistic and Structural Function
        of Names in the "Quijote." University
        of Iowa, 1971.

        A dissertation on names by Cervantes.

645   Kuhl, E. P.
        "Chaucer's Madame Eglantine,"
        Modern Language Notes, 60 (1945),
        325-6.

646   Kumahov, M. A.
        "K etimologii imeni osnovnogo geroja
        adygskogo i abhazskogo eposa," Skazanije
        o nartah-epos narodov Kavkaza. Moskva,
        1969.

        On names in Kaukasian epos, see particularly
        on "Sosryko" and on "Soslan." See pp.
        497-502.

647   Kuna, Franz
        Franz Kafka: Literature as Corrective
        Punishment. Bloomington, Indiana University
        Press, 1974.

        On the names "Sacher-Masoch" and "Samsa,"
        see pp. 36-7.

648   Kunitzsch, Paul
        "Die Planetennamen im 'Parzival',"
        Zeitschrift für deutsche Sprache, 25
        (1969), 169-74.

        On names of planets in Parzival.

649   Kurzowa, Z.
        "Meskie imiona zdrobniale i spieszczone
        w piesniach ludu polskiego (na podstawie
        Dziel wszystkich Oskara Kolberga),"
        Onomastica, 15 (1970), 234-81.

        On names in Polish folksongs..

650 Lachmann, Fritz, R.
  "Goethe's Mignon: Entstehung, Name,
  Gestaltung," Germanisch-romanische
  Monatsschrift, 15 (1927), 100-16.

  On the name "Mignon" by Goethe.

651 Lambert, Eloise, and Mario Pei
  Our Names. Where They Came from and What
  They Mean. New York, Lothrop, 1960.

  On personal names; general.

652 Lampe, Walther
  Vornamen und ihre Bedeutung. Eine
  Auswahl. 2nd ed. Frankfurt, Standesamtswesen,
  1968.

  On the meaning of first names.

  Lang, A.
    See: 414.

653 Langendonck, Willy van
  Bibliographia Onomastica 1971. Leuven,
  International Centre of Onomastics, 1974.

  Continued in Onoma on a yearly basis.
  See particularly "Literature and Names."

654 Langlois, Ernest
  Table des noms propres de toute nature
  compris dans les chansons de geste
  imprimées. Paris, Bouillon, 1904.

  On names in the chansons de geste.

655 Larzac, J.
  "Los noms balhats a Maria dins la
  literature e l'usatge occitans," Revue
  des Langues Romanes, 78 (1970), 419-48.

  On literary onomastics.

656 Laski, E. de
       "The Psychological Attitude of Charles
       Dickens Toward Surnames," The American
       Journal of Psychology, 29 (1918), 337-46.

657 Latham, Edward
       A Dictionary of Names, Nicknames, and Sur-
       names of Persons, Places, and Things. London,
       Routledge, 1904. Reprint: Detroit, Gale, 1966.

658 Latkovskis, L.
       "Literari tipi nusaukti pec edinim,"
       Dzeive (München), 3/60 (1963), 13.

       On names in the novels of Karlis Ievinš.

659 Laugesen, Anker Teilgard
       "Quelques remarques sur la valeur stylistique
       des noms de personnes," Communications, 32
       (1968-9).

       On the stylistic value of personal names.

660 Lausberg, Heinrich
       " A Review of Nellmann's 'Wolframs
       Erzähltechnik'," Beiträge zur Namenfor-
       schung, 12 (1977), 227-8.

     ---, See: 834.

661 Lauterbach, J. Z.
       "The Naming of Children in Jewish Folklore,
       Ritual, and Practice," Central Conference of
       American Rabbis Year-Book, 42 (1932), 316-60.

662 Law, R. A.
       "On Certain Proper Names in Shakespeare,"
       The University of Texas Studies in English,
       30 (1951), 61-5.

663 Lebel, Paul
        Les noms de personnes. Paris, Presses
        Universitaires de France, 1974.

        On personal names.

664 Lecoutere, C. P. F.
        "Onomasticon of lijst van PN der mndl.
        letterkunde," (Manauskript bei der
        Koniklijke Vlaamsche Akademie van
        Taal- en Letterkunde) Onoma, 1, 21.

        On personal names.

665 Lees, F. N.
        'Othello's Name," Notes and Queries, 8
        (1961), 139-41.

        On the name "Othello" by Shakespeare.

666 Le Guin, Ursula K.
        "The Rule of Names," in The Wind's Twelve
        Quarters. New York, Harper, 1975.

        On names in science fiction. See also
        Fantastic, 1963.

667 Lehiste, I.
        "Names of Scandinavians in the Anglo-Saxon
        Chronicle," Publications of the Modern
        Language Association, 73 (1958), 6-22.

668 Lehman, W. P.
        "Lin and laukr in the Edda," Germanic
        Review, 3 (1955), 1963-71.

669 Lejeune, R.
        Les Héros littéraires et l'anthroponymie
        mediévale. Salamanca, 1955.

        On personal names of literary heroes of
        the Middle Ages.

Le Scanff, Jacques
        See: 170.

670 Levi, P. Margot
        "K., an Exploration of the Names of
        Kafka's Central Characters," Names,
        14 (1966), 1-10.

671 Levin, Harry
        "Shakespeare's Nomenclature," in Essays
        on Shakespeare. Princeton, Princeton
        University Press, 1965.

        See pp. 59-90.

672 Levin, L. M.
        "Note on the Arouet>Voltaire Problem,"
        Studies in Philology, 34 (1937), 52-54.

673 Levin, Richard
        "Middleton's Way with Names in 'A Chaste
        Maid in Cheapside'," Notes and Queries, 210
        (1965), 102-3.

674 ---, "Name Puns in 'The Family of Love',"
        Notes and Queries, 210 (1965), 340-2.

        On names by Middleton.

675 ---, "Quomodo's Name in Michaelmas Term,"
        Notes and Queries, 20 (1973), 460-1.

        On the above name by Middleton.

676 Levith, Murray J.
        "Juliet's Question and Shakespeare's
        Names," in Renaissance and Modern Essays
        in Honor of Edwin M. Moseley. Ed. by
        Murray J. Levith. Skidmore College and
        Syracuse University Press, 1976.

        See pp. 21-32.

677 Levitt, Jesse
"Irony and Allusiveness in Gide's Onomastics,"
Literary Onomastics Studies, 3 (1976), 110-9.

678 --- "Names in Beckett's Theater: Irony and Mystifi
ation," Literary Onomastics Studies, 4 (1977),
49-64.

679 Leys, O.
"De eigennaam als linguistisch teken,"
Mededelingen van de Vereiniging voor
Naamkunde te Leuven en de Commissie voor
Naamkunde te Amsterdam, 41 (1965), 1-81.

On personal names and linguistics.

680 Lieb, M.
"Holy Name: A Reading of Paradise Lost,"
Harvard Theological Review, 67 (1974),
321-39.

On names by Milton.

681 Liljegren, S. B.
"Some Notes on the Name of James Harrington's
Oceana," in Probleme der englischen Sprache
und Kultur. Festschrift Johannes Hoops. Hrsg.
von Wolfgang Keller. Heidelberg, Winter, 1925
(Germanische Bibliothek, Untersuchungen und
Texte, 20)

682 Lindemans, Jan
"Onomastiek in dienst van de Literatuur-
geschiedenis," Verslagen en Mededelingen
der Koninklijke Klaamse Akademie voor
Taal- en Letterkunde (1941), 507-21.

On onomastics and literary history.

683 Lindsay, J.
"Horace or Horatius?" Bookman (London),
87 (1934), 188.

On variations in spelling of Greek and
Latin names.

684 Link, Manfred
    *Namen im Werk Thomas Manns: Deutung,
    Bedeutung, Funktion*, 1966. (The Pro-
    ceedings of the Department of Foreign
    Languages and Literatures, College of
    General Education. University of
    Tokyo, Vol. 14, No. 1)

    On the names in the works of Thomas Mann.

685 Linsky, Leonard
    Names and Descriptions. Chicago, University
    of Chicago Press, 1977.

    On semantics.

686 Lish, Terrence G.
    *Name Symbolism in Melville's "Pierre" and
    a Selected Onomastics Glossary for His
    Prose*. University of Nevada, 1971.

    A dissertation.

687 Lithgow, Douglas R. A.
    "The Orthography of Shakespeare's Name,"
    The Antiquary, 2 (1880), 190-4; 3 (1881),
    17-20.

688 Littger, Klaus Walter
    *Studien zum Auftreten der Heiligennamen
    im Rheinland*, 1975. (Münsterische Mittel-
    alter-Schriften, 20)

    See p. 239 on the names of saints in
    literature.

Littmann, Enno
    See: 929.

689 Liu, J. Y.
    "The Name of the Arabian King in Marlowe's
    Tamburlaine," *Notes and Queries*, 195 (1950), 10.

690 Lodemann, Jürgen
     "Thomas Mann und seine Namen," <u>Die Welt</u>,
     185 (12-8-1965), 5.

     On names in the works of Thomas Mann.

691 Loewer, Barry Monroe
     <u>Knowledge, Names, and Necessity</u>. Stanford
     University 1975.

     A dissertation.

692 Long, Harry Alfred
     <u>Personal and Family Names</u>. A popular
     monograph on the origin and history of
     the nomenclature of the present and former
     times. London, Hamilton, 1883. Reprint:
     Detroit, Gale, 1968.

693 Loomis, R. S.
     "Onomastic Riddles in Malory's Book of
     Arthur and His Knights," <u>Medium Aevum</u>,
     25 (1956), 181-90.

694 ---, "Some Names in Arthurian Romance,"
     <u>Publications of the Modern Language
     Association</u>, 45 (1930), 416-43.

695 Lopušanskaja-Bučko, A. E.
     "Struktura ličnogo imeni u Gomera,"
     <u>Antroponimika</u> (1970), 319-21.

     On personal names by Homer.

696 ---, "Struktura skladnych osobovych imen
     u Gomera," <u>Respublikanska Onomastyčna
     Konferencija Kyjiv</u>, 4 (1969), 196-8.

     On names by Homer.

697 Lőrincze, L, I. L. Markó, and E. Urban
     "Az irodalmi névadásról," <u>Magyar
     Nyelvőr</u>, 80 (1956), 198-204.

     On Hungarian literary onomastics.

698 Lotte, Fernand
Dictionnaire biographique des personnages
fictifs de La comédie humaine. Avec un
avant-propos de Marcel Bouteron. Paris,
Corti, 1952.

On Balzac's use of names. See also the
supplement: Personnages fictifs anonymes.
Paris, Corti, 1956.

699 Lower, Mark Anthony
The Book of English Surnames. Lewes, 1839.

700 ---, English Surnames. London, Smith, 1842.

See also later edition subtitled:
Essays on Family Nomenclature.

701 ---, Patronymica britannica. A Dictionary of
the Family Names of the United Kingdom.
London, Smith, 1860.

702 Lubas, W.
"Rola nazw wlasnych w stylistice sowizrzalskiej
(Na marginesie pracy S. Grzeszczuka, Nazewnictwo
sowizrzalskie)," Ruch Literacki, 11/2 (1970),
141-4.

On names in the works of S. Grzeszczuk.

Lübke, Wilhelm Meyer
See: Meyer-Lübke, Wilhelm

703 Luby, B. J.
"The Names of Christ in Fray Luis de León's
'De los nombres de Cristo'," Names, 18 (1970),
2-28.

704 Lucas, Edward Verrall
Luck of the Year: Essays, Fantasies,
and Stories. Freeport, Books for Libraries
Press, 1969. (Essay Index Reprint Series)

See pp. 53-60 on names. See also original
edition: 1923.

705 Luka, K.
        "Toponimia shqiptare nc Kangen e Rolandit
        me dis nglarje te vjeteve 1081-5," Studie
        historike. 21-4/2 (1967), 127-44.

        On toponyma in the "Chanson de Roland."

706 Lunzer, Justus
        "Zum Gebrauche' redender Namen," Beiträge
        zur Geschichte der deutschen Sprache und
        Literatur, 51 (1927), 190-5.

        On descriptive names in literature.

707 Luther, Martin
        Namen-Büchlein. Hrsg. von G. Wegener.
        Leipzig, 1674. Reprint: Leipzig, Zentral-
        antiquariat der DDR, 1974.

        An onomastic treatise originally called De
        aliquot nomina propria Germanorum ad
        priscam etymologiam restituta.

708 Maas, Herbert
      Von Abel bis Zwicknagel. Lexikon deutscher
      Familiennamen. München, Deutscher Taschenbuch
      Verlag, 1964. (dtv 255)

      A lexicon of German family names.

709 MacAndrew, Elizabeth M.
      "Fielding's Use of Names in Joseph Andrews,"
      Names, 16 (1968), 362-70.

710 McCartney, Eugene S.
      Pun and Plays on Names," Classical Journal,
      14 (1919), 343-58.

711 McClear, Margaret
      "Charactonyms in Miguel Angel Asturias'
      'Mulata de Tal'," in Naughty Names
      F. Tarpley, Commerce, Texas, Names Institute
      Press, 1975. (South Central Names Institute
      Publication No. 4)

      See pp. 39-44.

712 McDonnell, Helen Margaret
      A Study of the Names of Characters in
      Shakespearean Comedy. Rutgers University,
      1970.

      A dissertation.

713 McGarry, Francis de Sales
      The Allegorical and Metaphorical Language
      in the Autos sacramentales of Calderon.
      Washington, D. C., The Catholic University
      of America, 1937.

      A dissertation.

714 McGarry, Jim
      Place Names in the Writings of William
      Butler Yeats. Ed. and with additional
      material by Edward Malins; and a preface
      by Kathleen Raine. Gerrards Cross, Smythe,
      1976.

715   McInnes, J.
      "Personal Names in a Gaelic Song,"
      Scottish Studies, 6 (1962), 235-43.

716   MacLean, Hugh
      "Bassanio's Name and Nature," *Names*, 25
      (1977), 55-62.

      On above name by Shakespeare.

717   McMullen, Wallace E.
      "An Onomastic Review of Gilbert-Sullivan,"
      Literary Onomastics Studies, 1 (1974),
      28-39.

      MacNeill, Eoin
      See: 333.

718   Macurdy, G. H.
      "Homeric Names in 'tor', and Some Other
      Names of the Short Form Occurring in
      Homer," *Classical Quarterly*, 23 (1929),
      23-7.

      McWilliam, Richebourg Gaillard
      See: 976.

719   Madden, Frederic
      "Observations on an Autograph of Shakespere,
      and the Orthography of His Name," *Archaeologia*,
      27 (1837), 113-23.

720   ---, "Orthography of Shakspere - Ralegh -
      Burghley," *The Gentleman's Magazine*, 167
      (1840), 262-4.

721   Madyda, Wladyslaw
      "Etymologie poetyckie imion wlasnych
      u Homera," *Onomastica* (Wroclaw), 9
      (1964), 231-71.

      On names by Homer.

722 Magazanik, E. B.
      "Rol' antroponima v postroenii
      hudoẑestvennogo obraza," <u>Onomastika</u>
      (1969), 162-3.

      On the role of personal names in liter-
      ary works.

723 Magoun, Francis P.
      <u>A Chaucer Gazetteer</u>. Chicago, University
      of Chicago Press, 1961.

724 ---, "Geographical and Ethnic Names in the
      Nibelungenlied," <u>Mediaeval Studies</u>, 7
      (1945), 85-138.

725 Maher, Peter J.
      "English 'Davit'/Old French 'Daviet' and
      Modern French 'Davier': A Biblical Echo
      in Medieval Sailors' Speech (with Remarks
      on Semantic and Phonological Theory),"
      <u>Literary Onomastics Studies</u>, 1 (1974),
      22-7.

726 Mahood, Molly Maureen
      <u>Shakespeare's Word Play</u>. London, Methuen,
      1957.

727 Maier, John R.
      "Mesopotamian Names in 'The Sunlight
      Dialogues'; or, MAMA Makes it to Batavia,
      New York," <u>Literary Onomastics Studies</u>,
      4 (1977), 33-48.

      On names by John Gardner.

728 ---, "What Happened to Sam-Kha in 'The Epic of
      Gilgames'?" <u>Literary Onomastics Studies</u>,
      2 (1975), 83-99.

729   Majtánová, M.
"Vlastni jména osob v národních báchorkách
a pověstech Boženy Němcové," <u>Zpravodaj
Místnopisné Komise Československé Akademie
Věd</u>, 12 (1971), 377-87.

On folklore names in the works of the
Czech writer B. Němcová.

Malins, Edward
    See: 714.

730   Malone, Kemp
"Meaningful Fictive Names in English Literature," <u>Names</u>, 5 (1957), 1-13.

731   ---, "A Review of Karl Schneider's 'Die germanischen Runennamen'," <u>Names</u>, 9 (1961), 129-35.

---, See: 1035.

732   ---, "A Review of Kökeritz's 'Shakespeare's
Names'," <u>Shakespeare Quarterly</u>, 11 (1960),
207-9.

---, See: 613.

733   ---, "Royal Names in Old English Poetry,"
<u>Names</u>, 1 (1953), 153-62.

734   Mancing, Howard
"The Comic Function of Chivalric Names in
'Don Quijote'," <u>Names</u>, 21 (1973), 220-35.

On names by Cervantes.

Mandel, Jerome
    See: 820.

735 Manfred, Frederick
        "A Note on Choice of Names," Names, 14
        (1966), 247-8.

        On names in his "Boy Almighty."

     Manheim, Ralph
        See: 169.

736 Manly John M.
        Some New Light on Chaucer. Lecture
        delivered at the Lowell Institute.
        New York, Holt, 1926.

        See pp. 80-1 on names. See also
        later edition, 1951.

737 Marchand, J. W.
        "Names of Germanic Origin in Latin
        and Romance Sources in the Study of
        Germanic Phonology," Names, 7 (1959),
        167-81.

738 Margocsy, J.
        Adalékok a XX. századi humoros-szatirikus
        irodalmi névadás történetéhez," Nyelvtudományi
        Értekezések, 70 (1970), 171-6.

        On Hungarian humorous and satirical literary
        onomastics of the twentieth century.

     Markó, I. L.
        See: 697.

     Marte-San
        See: San-Marte

739 Martin, R. H.
        "The Prosody of Greek Proper Names in -A
        in Plautus and Terence," The Classical
        Quarterly, 5 (1955), 206-9.

740 Martin, R. M., and Schotch, P. K.
"The Meaning of Fictional Names,"
Philosophical Studies, 26 (1974),
377-88.

741 Masani, Ruston Pestonji
Folk Culture Reflected in Names.
Bombay, Popular Prakashan, 1966.

742 Maschietto, Julianus
Onomasticon Ovidianum. Patavii, Livianis,
1970. (Scriptorum Romanorum quae extant
omnia, 168)

On names by P. Ovidius Naso.

743 Matic, T.
"Motiv Genovene u starijoj hrvatskoj
književnosti," Grada za povijest
književnosti hrvatske, 29 (1968), 41-101.

On the motif of Genovene in Old Croatian
literature.

744 Matthes, H. C.
"A Review of G. Storms' 'Compound Names ...',"
Anglia, 80 (1962-3), 168-70.

On names in "Beowulf."

---, See: 1167.

745 Matthews, Brander
"On the Poetry of Place-Names," in Parts
of Speech; Essays on English. New York,
Scribner, 1901.

See pp. 271-91.

746 Matthews, Constance Mary (Carrington)
English Surnames. New York, Scribner,
1967.

On English personal names.

747 ---, <u>How Surnames Began</u>. London, Lutter-
        worth. 1967.

        See also the 1977 edition.

748 Matthews, W.
        "Where Was Siesia-Sessoyne?" <u>Speculum</u>, 49
        (1974), 680-6.

        On the above toponym by Geoffrey.

749 Matthias, Walther
        "Zur Deutung des Namens der Nibelungen,"
        <u>Germanisch-romanische Monatsschrift</u>, 7
        (1919), 333-6.

        On the name Nibelungen.

750 Maurer, Warren R.
        "Another View of Literary Onomastics. A
        Reply to H. Kratz," <u>Names</u>, 11 (1963),
        106-14.

        On names by Thomas Mann.

751 ---, "Names From 'The Magic Mountain'," <u>Names</u>,
        9 (1961), 248-59.

        On names by Thomas Mann.

     ---, See: 628, 873.

752 Mawson, Christopher Orlando Sylvester
        <u>International Book of Names</u>. A dictionary
        of the more difficult proper names in liter-
        ature, history, philosophy, religion, art,
        music, and other studies, together with the
        official form and pronunciation of the
        names of present-day celebrities and places
        throughout the world, with post-war geo-
        graphical changes duly incorporated. New
        York, Crowell, 1934.

                        .

753 Maxwell, J. C.
     "The Name of Brutus," <u>Notes and Queries</u>,
     212 (1967), 136.

     On the above name by Shakespeare.

754 Mayers, William Frederick
     <u>The Chinese Reader's Manual</u>. A handbook of
     biographical, historical, mythological, and
     general literary reference. Shanghai,
     American Presbyterian Mission Press, 1910.
     Reprint: Detroit, Gale, 1968.

     Originally published in 1874.

     Mayhew, A. L.
     See: 145.

755 Maync, Harry
     "Nomen et omen. Von bürgerlicher und
     dichterischer Namengebung," <u>Westermanns
     Monatshefte</u>, 62 (1917-8), 653-64.

     On names in German literature ranging from
     Goethe to E. T. A. Hoffman.

756 Mayrhofer, Manfred
     "Namen aus Persepolis und Susan,"
     <u>Mélanges linguistiques offerts à Emile
     Benveniste. Collection Linguistique</u>,
     70 (1975), 415-8.

     On names in "Persepolis" and "Susan".

757 ---, <u>Onomastica Persepolitana</u>. Das altiranische
     Namengut der Persepolis Täfelchen ... Wien,
     Österreichische Akademie der Wissenschaften,
     1973. (Österreichische Akademie der Wissen-
     schaften, Philologisch-historische Klasse.
     Sitzungsberichte, Bd. 286)

     On Old Persian names.

758   ---, "Zu einer Deutung des Zarathustra-Namens
       in Nietzsches Korrespondenz," in Beiträge
       zur alten Geschichte und deren Nachleben.
       Festschrift für Franz Altheim und Hans
       Erich Stier. 2 vols. Berlin, de Gruyter,
       1970.

       On Nietzsche's name "Zarathustra," see pp.
       369-74.

       Meertens, P. J.
           See: 984.

       Meid, Wolfgang
           See: 609, 997, 1175.

759   Meier, Arnold
           Die alttestamentische Namengebung in England.
           Mit einem Ausblick auf die alttestamentliche
           Namengebung in Deutschland und Frankreich.
           Leipzig, Tauchnitz, 1934. (Kölner anglistische
           Arbeiten, Bd. 22)

           On name giving in the Old Testament in England,
           Germany, and France.

760   Meinecke, D.
           Wort und Name bei Paul Celan. Zur Widerruf-
           lichkeit des Gedichts. Würzburg, 1970.

           A dissertation on word and name by Celan.

761   Melchers, Paul
           "Die Bedeutung des Konrad Celtis für die
           Namenforschung," in Namenforschung. Fest-
           schrift für Adolf Bach zum 75. Geburtstag
           am 31. Januar 1965. Hrsg. von Rudolf
           Schützeichel und Matthias Zender. Heidelberg,
           Winter, 1965.

           On literary onomastics, see pp. 160-7.

       ---, See: 1269.

762   Mencken, Henry Louis
      The American Language. An inquiry into the
      development of English in the United States.
      New York, Knopf, 1936.

      On "Proper Names in America," see pp.
      474-554. See also the later edition.

763   Mendelsohn, Charles Jastrow
      The Name Play in Plautus. University of
      Pennsylvania, 1904.

      A dissertation.

764   Menéndez Pidal, Ramón
      La Chanson de Roland y el neotradicionalismo
      (Origines de la épica románica). Madrid,
      Espasa-Calpe, 1959.

      On names in the "Chanson de Roland."

      ---, See: 8.

765   Menke, Hubertus
      Die Tiernamen in Van den Vos Reinaerde.
      Heidelberg, Winter, 1970. (Beiträge zur
      Namenforschung, Beiheft, No. 6)

      On animal names in the Reinaert tradition.

766   Mensching, E.
      "A Review of D. C. Swanson's 'The Names in
      Roman Verse'," Indogermanische Forschungen,
      74 (1969), 278-83.

      ---, See: 1182.

767   Meritt, B. D.
      "The Name of Sophokles," American Journal
      of Philology, 80 (1959), 189.

768   Merlingen, W.
      "Zu einem Ortsnamen in den Pylos-Texten
      von 1960," Die Sprache, 8 (1962), 263.

      On a place-name in the Pylos texts.

769   Meyer-Lübke, Wilhelm
      "Romanische Namenstudien," Kaiserliche
      Akademie der Wissenschaften. Philosophisch-
      historische Klasse, 149/2 (1905), 1-102.

      On Romance names.

770   Meyer, Richard M.
      "Apologie des Namenwitzes," Nation, 19
      (1903), 518-21.

      On plays on names.

771   ---, Die deutsche Literatur des neunzehnten
      Jahrhunderts. 3. Aufl. Berlin, Bondi,
      1906. (Das neunzehnte Jahrhundert in
      Deutschlands Entwicklung, Bd. 3)

      On German literary onomastics, passim.

      Meyer, W. Tobler
      See: Tobler-Meyer, W.

772   Meyers, Walter E.
      "'The Dispossessed' and How They Got to be
      That Way: Ursula K. Le Guin's Onomastics,"
      Names, 25 (1977), 115-8.

773   Meyerson, E.
      "Note on they Etymology of Names in Voltaire's
      Zadig," Modern Language Notes, 54 (1939), 597-8.

774   Michajlov, V. N.
      "Rol' sobstvennych imen v proizvedijach N. V.
      Gogolja," Russkij jazyk v škole, 15/2 (1954),
      40-8.

      On proper names in Gogol's work.

775   Mieder, Wolfgang
      "International Bibliography of Explanatory
      Essays on Proverbs and Proverbial Expressions
      Containing Names," Names, 24 (1976), 253-304.

776 Mieszkowszki, G.
"Pandras in Deschamps' Ballade for
Chaucer," Chaucer Review, 9 (1975),
327-36.

777 Migliorini, B.
Dal nome proprio al nome comune. Studi
semantici sul mutamento dei nomi propri di
persona in nomi comuni negl'idiomi romanzi.
Genève, Olschki, 1927. (Bibliotheca dell
Archivum romanicum. Ser. II. Linguistica,
Vol. 13)

On proper and common names in Romance
languages.

778 Miklosich, F.
"Die Bildung der slavischen Personennamen,"
Deutsch-Schriften der K. K. Akademie der
Wissenschaften zu Wien. Philosophisch-
historische Klasse, 10 (1860), 215-330.

On Slavic personal names.

779 Mileck, J.
"Names and the Creative Process. A Study
of the Names in Hermann Hesse's 'Lauscher',
'Demian', 'Steppenwolf', and 'Glasperlenspiel',
Monatshefte für deutschen Unterricht, 53 (1961)
167-80.

780 Mill, John Stuart
System of Logic, Ratiocinative and Inductive.
Being a connected view of the principles of
evidence and the methods of scientific investigation. New York, Harper, 1868.

See pp. 15-30 "On Names," see also "Of
Things Denoted by Names."

781 Miller, E. M.
"Molière and His Homonym Louis de Mollier,"
Moder Language Notes, 74 (1959), 612-21.

782 Miller, John C.
    "Onomatology of Male Characters in the 'One
    Hundred Years of Solitude' of Gabriel García
    Marques," <u>Literary Onomastics Studies</u>, 1
    (1974), 66-73.

    Includes also family tree.

783 Miller, J. H.
    "Ariachne's Broken Woof," <u>Georgia Review</u>,
    31 (1977), 44-60.

    On "Troilus and Cressida" by Shakespeare.

784 Miller, L.
    "A Reply to Colwell's Huckleberry Finn,"
    <u>Publications of the Modern Language
    Association</u>, 87 (1972), 314.

    On names by M. Twain.

785 Miso-Shak (pseud.)
    "Barbarism of Mis-Spelling Shakespeare's
    Name," <u>The Gentleman's Magazine</u>, 57 (June
    1787), 478.

786 Moffett, James Mark
    <u>A Name, Works, and Selected Subjects Index
    of the Correspondence of John Gould Fletcher
    for Correspondents 'L' Through 'Z'</u>. Uni-
    versity of Arkansas, 1968.

    A dissertation. For "A" through "K", see
    Peters, O. L.

---, See: 901.

Moldovej, Ceril
    See: 566.

787 Moll, Otto
    <u>Sprichwörterbibliographie</u>. Frankfurt,
    Klostermann, 1958.

    A bibliography on proverbs.

788 Monaco, M.
"Racine's Naming of Greek Confidantes and
Handmaids," Romanic Review, 52 (1961), 99-115.

789 Montaigne, Michel Eyquemde
"Of Names," in The Essays of Montaigne. Tr.
by E. J. Trenchmann. 2 vols. New York,
Oxford University Press, 1946.

See vol. 1, pp. 269-74. See also the
original edition: Ensayos de Montaigne.
2 vols. Paris, Garnier, 1898.

790 Monteith, Robert
"Illustration of the Proper Names," The
Very Learned Scotsman. Mr. George Buchanan's
Fratres fraterrimi, three books of epigrams,
and book of miscellanies, in English verse,
with the illustration of the proper names,
and mythologies therein mentioned. Edinburgh, Anderson, 1708.

On Greek and Latin names.

791 Montenegro, A.
La onomástica de Virgilio y la antigüedad
preitálica, Salamanca, 1949.

An onomasticon on Vergil.

792 Montgomery, Edward D.
"Tartuffe: The History and Sense of a
Name," Modern Language Notes, 88 (1973),
838-40.

On names by Molière.

793 Mook, Maurice A.
"A Review of J. W. Freeman's 'Discovering
Surnames ...'." Names, 18 (1970), 118-9.

---, See: 342.

794 Moore, Marianne
     A Marianne Moore Reader. New York, Viking,
     1961.

     On names, see pp. 215-24.

795 Moravcevich, J.
     "Racine's Andromaque and the Rhetoric of
     Naming," Papers on Language and Literature,
     12 (1976), 20-35.

796 Moravcsik, Gy.
     "Zur Frage der Chinove im Igor-Lied,"
     Journal of Slavic Linguistics and Poetics,
     3 (1960), 69-72.

     On names in the "Igor-Lied."

797 Morby, E. S.
     "A Review of 'Los nombres ...' by
     Morley-Tyler," Romanic Philology, 17
     (1963), 511-6.

     On names by Lope de Vega.

     ---, See: 802.

798 Moreno, Teresa Garcia
     "The Old and the New: The Onomastics of
     an Argentinian Picaresque Novel," Literary
     Onomastics Studies, 4 (1977), 65-80.

     On names by Guidino Kieffer.

799 Morland, H.
     "Zu den Namen in der Aeneis," Symboloe
     Osloenses, 36 (1960), 21-9.

     On names by Homer.

800 Morley, Sylvanus Griswold
     "Arabic Nomenclature in the Characters of
     Lope de Vega's Plays," University of
     California Publications, Semitic Philology,
     11 (1951), 339-43.

801 ---, "Character Names in Tirso de Molina,"
       Hispanic Review, 27 (1959), 222-7.

802 ---, and Richard W. Tyler
       Los nombres de personajes en las comedias
       de Lope de Vega; estudio de onomatologia.
       2 vols. Berkeley, University of California
       Press, 1961. (University of California
       Publications in Modern Philology, Vol. 55,
       No. 1-2)

       On names by Lope de Vega.

       ---, See: 46, 53, 797, 955, 1265, 1266.

803 Morovic, H.
       "Legenda o Aleksiju u starijoj hrvatskoj
       književnosti," Grada za povijest književ-
       nosti hrvatske, 29 (1968), 433-79.

       On names in the Alexis legend, Old Croatian
       literature.

804 Morris, H.
       "Richard Barnfield, Amyntas, and the
       Sidney Circle," Publications of the Modern
       Language Association, 74 (1959), 318-24.

       On names by R. Barnfield and others.

       ---, See: 1139.

805 Morris, John
       "The Name of Shakespeare," The Journal
       of English and Germanic Philology, 30
       (1931), 578-80.

     Moseley, Ann
       See: 69, 74, 144, 221, 382, 1072, 1114,
       1151, 1192, 1198, 1203, 1242.

     Moseley, Edwin M.
       See: 676.

806 Mossé, F.
          "Anthroponomie et histoire littéraire:
          le Roman de Renart dans 'Angleterre du
          Moyen Age'," Les Languages Modernes,
          45 (1951), 70-84.

          On personal names and the history of
          literature of the Middle Ages.

807 Muhamedova, Z. B., and Ahally, S.
          "Toponimy v lirike nekotoryh turkmenskih
          poetov," Top Vost, (1969), 99-112.

          On toponyma in the lyrics of Turkmenian
          poets.

808 Mühlestein, H.
          "Redende Personennamen bei Homer,"
          Studi Micenei ed Egeo-anatolici, 9
          (1969), 67-94.

          On descriptive personal names by Homer.

809 Müllenhoff, Karl
          "Zeugnisse und Excurse zur deutschen
          Heldensage," Zeitschrift für deutsches
          Altertum, 12 (1965), 253-86, and 413-36.

          On onoma tics in German heroic literature.

810 Müller, Eugen Hartmut
          "Deutung einiger Namen im Nibelungenlied,"
          Monatshefte für deutschen Unterricht, deutsche
          Sprache und Literatur, 31 (1939), 274-84.

          On names in the Nibelungen.

811 Müller, Friedrich Max
          Contributions to the Science of Mythology.
          2 vols. London, Longmans, 1897.

          On mythological names, passim.

812 ---, Natural Religion. The Gifford lectures delivered before the University of Glasgow in 1888. London, Longmans, 1889.

See pp. 476-83: "Nomina and cognomina."

813 Müller, Gunter
Studien zu den theriophoren Personennamen der Germanen. Köln, Böhlau, 1970. (Niederdeutsche Studien, Bd. 17)

On Germanic theriophoric names.

814 Müller, Richard
"Beiträge zur Geschichte der mittel-hochdeutschen Literatur in Österreich," Zeitschrift für deutsches Altertum und deutsche Literatur, 31 (1887), 82-103.

On names in Middle High German literature.

815 Murphy, G. N.
"A Note on Iago's Name," in Literature and Society by Germaine Bree and others. Ed. by Bernice Slote. A selection of papers delivered at the joint meeting of the Midwest Modern Language Association and the Central Renaissance Conference, 1963. Lincoln, University of Nebraska Press, 1964. (A Bison book)

See pp. 38-43 on the above name by Shakespeare.

816 Murphy, W. F.
"A Note on the Significance of Names," Psychoanalytic Quarterly, 26 (1957), 91-106.

817 Muscatine, Charles
"The Names of Chaucer's Friar," Modern Language Notes, 70 (1955), 169-72.

818 Musculus, Carl Theodor
Inhalts- und Namen-Verzeichnis über
sämmtliche Goethe'sche Werke. Nach der
Ausgabe letzter Hand und dem Nachlasse
verfertigt. Stuttgart, 1835. Reprint:
Leipzig, Zentralantiquariat der DDR, 1976.

Index to subjects and names in the works
of Goethe.

819 Musgrove, S.
"The Nomenclature of King Lear," Review of
English Studies, 7 (1956), 294-8.

On names by Shakespeare.

820 Mustanoja, Tauno F.
"The Suggestive Use of Christian Names in
Middle English Poetry," in Medieval Literature and Folklore Studies. Essays in
honor of Francis Lee Utley. Ed. by Jerome
Mandel and Bruce A. Rosenberg. New Bruns-
wick, Rutgers University Press, 1970.

See pp. 51-76.

821 Myers, John Vernon
Jehan de Lanson. Chanson de geste of the
Thirteenth Century. Ed. after the manuscripts of Paris and Bern with introduction,
variants, notes, table of proper names,
and glossary. University of North Carolina
at Chapel Hill, 1959.

A dissertation.

822   Name in Sprache und Gesellschaft. Beiträge
      zur Theorie der Onomastik. Hrsg. von
      Hans Walther. Berlin, Akademie Verlag,
      1973. (Deutsch-slawische Forschungen
      zur Namenkunde und Siedlungsgeschichte,
      Nr. 27)

      On the theory of onomastics.

823   Namenforschung. Festschrift für Adolf Bach zum
      50. Geburtstag am 31. January 1965. Hrsg.
      von Rudolf Schützeichel und Matthias Zender.
      Heidelberg, Winter, 1965.

      A collection of essays on German onomastics.

824   Namenforschung heute. Ihre Ergebnisse und
      Aufgaben in der DDR. Von einem Autorenkol-
      lektiv. Berlin, Akademie Verlag, 1971.

      On German onomastics - its results and
      its goals.

825   Namenschlüssel zu Pseeudonymen, Doppelnamen und
      Namenabwandlungen. Bearb. von einem
      Kollektiv der Deutschen Staatsbibliothek,
      Berlin, Hrsg. von Elisabeth Lotte von Oppen.
      Hildesheim, Olms, 1968.

      Keys to pseudonyms, hyphenated, and varied
      names.

826   Nanavutty, Piloo (pseud.)
      "Puzzling Names in Blake," The Times
      Literary Supplement (July 3, 1937),
      496.

827   Narveson, Robert
      "The Name 'Claggart' in 'Billy Budd',"
      American Speech, 43 (1968), 229-32.

      On the above name by Melville.

828 Nathan, N.
"'Abram' not 'Abraham' in 'The Merchant of Venice'," Notes and Queries, 17 (1970), 127-8.

On the above name by Shakespeare.

829 ---, "The Goodwins - an Appropriate Name," Names, 7 (1959), 191-2.

On the above name by Shakespeare.

830 Naugle, Helen H.
"Name Bildad," Modern Fiction Studies, 22 (1976-7), 591-4.

On the above name by Sherwood Anderson.

Naumann, Hans
See: 601.

831 Naumann, Horst
"Nummer und Name. Diskussionsbeitrag zur Theorie des Eigennamens," Namenkundliche Informationen, 27 (1975), 6-16.

On numbers and names; particularly on the theory of proper names.

832 ---, "Zur Fragen moderner Namengebung," Wissenschaftliche Zeitschrift der Karl-Marx-Universität, Leipzig. Geschichtliche und sprachwissenschaftliche Reihe, H. 2, 13 (1964), 387-90.

On modern name giving, general.

833 Neider, Charles
The Frozen Sea. A Study of Franz Kafka. New York Russell, 1962.

See pp. 148-52 on "Nomenclature."

834 Nellmann, Eberhard
      Wolframs Erzähltechnik. Untersuchungen
      zur Funktion des Erzählers. Wiesbaden,
      Steiner, 1973.

      On the technique of narration by Wolfram,
      passim on names.

      ---, See: 660.

835 Neugaard, Edward Joseph
      A Critical Edition of a Portion of the
      Thirteenth Century "Vides de Sants
      Rosselloneses". With introduction,
      notes, table of proper names and
      glossary. University of North Carolina
      at Chapel Hill, 1964.

      A dissertation.

836 Neumann, Günter
      "Horst - ein Pferdename," Beiträge zur
      Namenforschung, 8 (1973), 343-4.

      On the above name by Klopstock, Klinger,
      Kleist, and Wieland.

837 Neveleva, S. L.
      "Epičeskaja onomastika (Opyt opisanija
      struktury)," Tez Lovian, 5 (1969), 142-4.

      On names in Old Indian epics.

838 New Century Cyclopedia of Names. Ed. by
      Clarence L. Barnhart with the assist-
      ance of William D. Halsey and a staff
      of more than 350 consulting scholars,
      special editors, and other contributors.
      3 vols. New York, Appleton, 1954.

839 Newcomer, Charles A.
      Animal Names in the Works of Alfonso el
      Sabio. Case Western Reserve University,
      1937.

      A dissertation.

Nicol, R.
        See: 488.

840 Nicolaisen, W. F. H.
        "Place-Name Legends: An Onomastic
        Mythology," Folklore, 87 (1976), 146-59.

        On localization of migratory legends.

841 ---, "Place-Names in Traditional Ballads,"
        Literary Onomastics Studies, 1 (1974),
        84-102.

842 ---, "The Place-Names of Barsetshire,"
        Literary Onomastics Studies, 3 (1976),
        1-21.

        On names by Anthony Trollope.

843 ---, "The Place-Names of Wessex," Literary
        Onomastics Studies, 2 (1975), 58-82.

        On names by Thomas Hardy.

844 ---, Scottish Place-Names: Their Study and
        Significance. London, Batsford, 1976.

845 Nicoloff, Assen
        Bulgarian Folklore, Folk Beliefs, Customs,
        Folksongs, Personal Names. Cleveland,
        1975.

846 Nikitin, V. M.
        "Stilistika ličnych imen v poezii N. A.
        Nekrasova," Onomastika Povolž'ja, 2 (1971),
        319-21.

        On names by Nekrasov.

847 Nikolaeva, Z. V.
        "Nabliudenija nad otčestvami v russkoj
        literature," Respublikanska Onomastyčna
        Konferencija, Kyjiv, 4 (1969), 140-2.

        On patronymics in Russian literature.

848 ---, "Naricatel'nye slova iz imen sobstvennich
i sobstvennye imena iz naricatel'nych v
poetičeskih proizvedenijach N. A. Nekrasova,"
Voprosy Russkogo Jazyka, 6 (1970), 181-91.

On proper names in the works of Nekrasov.

849 ---, "Otčestva personažej v poetičeskich
proizvedenijach N. A. Nekrasova, ich
stilistika, slovoobrazovanie i proizno-
senie," Voprosy Russkogo Jazyka, 6 (1970),
192-204.

On stylistics, structures, and pronoun-
ciations of personal names by Nekrasov.

850 Nikonov, V. A.
Imja i obshestvo. (Name and Society.)
Moscow, Science, 1974.

See the chapter on "The Names of Literary
Characters."

---, See: 1259.

851 Nitze, William Z.
"Additional Note on Arthurian Names,"
Publications of the Modern Language
Association, 65 (1950), 1287-8.

852 ---, "Arthurian Names: Arthur," Publications of
The Modern Language Association, 64 (1949),
585-6.

853 ---, Arthurian Names in the Perceval of
Chrétien de Troyes. Analysis and
commentary. By William A. Nitze and
Harry F. Williams. Berkeley University
of California Press, 1955. (University
of California Publications in Modern
Philology, Vol. 38, No. 3)

See pp. 265-97.

854 ---, "More on the Arthuriana of Nennius,"
Modern Language Notes, 58 (1943), 1-8.

855 Niva, Weldon N.
      "No-Names in Literature," <u>Names</u>, 12
      (1964), 89-97.

856 ---, "Significant Character Names in English
      Drama 1603," <u>Names</u>, 8 (1960), 180-1.

      An abstract.

857 ---, <u>Significant Character Names in English</u>
      <u>Drama to 1603</u>. University of Pennsylvania,
      1959.

      A dissertation.

858 Noel-Bentley, E. R.
      "Jane Austen and Regina Marie Roche,"
      <u>Notes and Queries</u>, 22 (1975), 390-1.

859 "Nomen est omen," <u>Books Abroad</u>, 18 (1944),
      242-3.

      On the names of German writers and their
      subjects.

860 Notopoulos, James A.
      "Name of Plato," <u>Classical Philology</u>, 34
      (1939), 135-45.

861 Nováková-Šlajsová, M.
      "A Review of V. Dmitriev's 'Pod vymyšlen-
      nymi ...'," <u>Zpravodaj Komise Československé</u>
      <u>Akademie Věd</u>, 11 (1970) 118-20.

      On Russian literary onomastics.

      ---, See: 251.

862 Nurmekund, P.
      "Miks Rabindranath Tagore?" <u>Keel ja</u>
      <u>Kirjandus</u>, (1961), 629.

      On the spelling of the above name.

863   Oberndorf, Clarence P.
        "Reaction to Personal Names," Psycho-
        analytical Review, 5 (1918), 47-52.

864   Ó Dubhagáin, Seán
        Topographical Poems. By Seaán Mór O
        Dubhagáin and Giolla-na-naomh O Huidhrin.
        Ed. by James Carney. Dublin, Institute
        for Advanced Studies, 1943.

        On names in Irish poems.

865   Oelrich, W.
        Die Personennamen im mittelalterlichen
        Drama Englands. Kiel University, 1911.

        A dissertation. On personal names in
        dramas of the Middle Ages in England.

866   O'Hara, John
        "If the Name Fits," Holiday, 41 (1967),
        28, and 30-1.

        On appropriate names in fiction.

867   Ohly, Friedrich
        "Synagoge und Ecclesia. Typologisches
        in mittelalterlicher Dichtung im Judentum
        im Mittelalter," Beiträge zum christlich-
        jüdischen Gespräch. Miscellanea Mediavelia.
        Veröffentlichungen des Thomas Institutes an
        der Universität Köln, 4 (1966), 1-406.

        On religious typology in the Middle Ages.

        O Hudhrin, Giolla-na-naomh
           See: 864.

868   Okada, S.
        Iseutamakura. Tsu, Publication de la
        Société d'Histoire Locale de la Préfecture
        de Mie, 1971.

        On toponyma in ancient Japanese poems.

Olberg, Hermann, M.
    See: 609, 997, 1175.

869 Oliver, Clinton Forrest
        The Name and Nature of American Negro
        Literature. An Interpretative Study
        in Genre and Ideas. Harvard Univer-
        sity, 1965.

        A dissertation.

Oppen, Elisabeth Lotte von
    See: 825.

870 O'Regan, M. J.
        "Genealogical Periphrases in Racine,"
        French Studies, 16 (1962), 14-23.

871 Orelli, Johann Kaspar von
        Onomasticon Tullianum, contens M. Tullii
        Ciceronis vitam, historiam litterariam ...
        1836. Reprint: Hildesheim, Olms, 1965.

        On names by M. T. Cicero.

872 Orosa, Rosalinda L.
        What's in a (Nick)name? Manila, Solidaridad,
        1969.

873 Ostberg, D. R.
        "A Reply to W. R. Maurer's Article on the
        Names by Thomas Mann," Names, 10 (1962),
        228.

---, See: 751.

874 Oyarzun, Luis A.
        "Some Functions of Names in Galdós's
        Novels," Literary Onomastics Studies,
        1 (1974), 74-83.

875 Paap, A. H. R. E.
Nomina sacra in the Greek Papyri of the
First Five Centuries A. D. The Sources
and Some Deductions. Leiden, Brill,
1959. (Papyrologica Lugduno-Botava,
Vol. 8)

876 Paff, William J.
The Geographical and Ethnic Names in the
"Thithriks Saga". A Study in the Old
Germanic Heroic Legend. Harvard Univer-
sity, 1950.

A dissertation.

877 ---, The Geographical and Ethnic Names of the
Pidriks Saga. A Study in Germanic Heroic
Legend. 's Gravenhagen, Mouton, 1959.

878 Pais, D.
"Aranyosrákosi Székely Sándor Székely
eposzának tündérmozzanatai," Studia
Litteraria (Debrezin), 5 (1967), 25-7.

On names in the Hungarian epos of S.
S. Aranyosrákosi.

879 Palomar Lapesa, Manuel
La onomastica personal pre-latina de la
antiqua Lusitania; estudio lingüistico.
Salamanca, Nebrija, 1957. (Theses et
studia philologica Salamanticensia, 10)

On Pre-Latin personal names.

880 Panzer, Friedrich
"Personennamen aus dem höfischen Epos in
Baiern," in Philosophische Studien. Festgabe
für Eduard Sievers zum 1. Oktober 1893.
Halle, Niemeyer, 1896.

On personal names in the courtly epos of
Bavaria, see pp. 205-20.

881   ---, "Der Weg der Nibelunge," <u>Erbe der</u>
<u>Vergangenheit</u>. Germanistische Beiträge.
Festgabe für Karl Helm zum 80. Geburtstag 19. Mai, 1951. Tübingen, Niemeyer, 1951.

On toponyma in the Nibelungen, see pp.
83-107.

882   Pape, Wilhelm, and G. Benseler
<u>Wörterbuch der griechischen Eigennamen</u>.
2 vols. Reprint of the 3rd ed. 1911.
Graz, Akademische Druck und Verlagsan-
stalt, 1959. (Orbis litterarum)

A dictionary of Greek first names.
Originally published as <u>Handwörterbuch</u>
<u>der griechischen Sprache</u>。

883   Parker, Alfred J。
<u>What's in Your Name? You Are Your Name</u>.
Vancouver, (n. p.) 1961.

884   Parthey, Gustav Friedrich Constantin
<u>Aegyptische Personennamen bei den</u>
<u>Klassikern, in Papyrusrollen, auf</u>
<u>Inschriften</u>. Berlin, Nicolai, 1864.

On Egyptian personal names.

885   Partridge, Eric
<u>Name Into Word. Proper Names that Have</u>
<u>Become Common Property</u>. A discursive
dictionary. 2nd edition revised and
enlarged, 1950. Reprint: Freeport,
Books for Libraries, 1970.

886   ---, <u>Name this Child</u>. A Dictionary of Modern
British and American Given or Christian
Names. 3rd edition revised and enlarged.
London, Hamilton, 1951.

887 Pasco, A. H.
          Marcel, Albertine and Balbec in Proust's
          Allusive Complex," _Romanic Review_, 62
          (1971), 113-26.

888 ---, and Wilfred J. Rollman
          "The Artistry of Gide's Onomastics," _Modern
          Language Notes_, 86 (1971), 523-31.

889 Pate, Frances Willard
          Names of Characters in Faulkner's Mississippi.
          Emory University, 1969.

          A dissertation.

890 Pauls, John P.
          "Chekhov's Humorous Names," _Literary
          Onomastics Studies_, 1 (1974), 53-65.

891 ---, "Chekhov's Names," _Names_, 23 (1975), 67-73.

892 ---, "Names for Characters in Russian Liter-
          ature," _Names_, 11 (1963), 10-9.

893 Pearce, S. M.
          "Cornish Elements in the Arthurian
          Tradition," _Folklore_, 85 (1974),
          145-63.

894 Pearsall, R. B.
          "Chaucer's Panic. (Clerk's Tale, 590),"
          Modern Language Notes, 67 (1952), 529-31.

895 Pechey, R. F.
          "Dickensian Nomenclature," _The Dickensian_,
          52 (1956), 180-2.

896 Peck, Harry Thurston
          "Names," _The Bookman_, 8 (1898), 334-8.

          On names in novels.

Pei, Mario
        See: 651.

897   Penzl, Herbert
        "Early Germanic Names and Vowel Shifts,"
        Names, 14 (1966), 65-8.

898   Penzoldt, Ernst
        "Magie der Namen," Westermanns Monatshefte,
        93 (1952-3), 20-1.

        On the magic of names.

899   Peppler, Charles William
        Comic Terminations in Aristophanes and the
        Fragments Part I.   Dimunitives, Character
        Names, Patronymies.   Johns Hopkins Univer-
        sity, 1898.

        A dissertation.

900   Peter, Hans Armin
        Thomas Mann und seine epische Charakteri-
        sierungskunst.   Bern, Haupt, 1929.
        (Sprache und Dichtung, Heft 43)

        On names by Thomas Mann, see pp. 74-80.

901   Peters, Oliver Leon
        A Name, Works, and Selected Subjects Index
        of the Correspondence of John Gould Fletcher
        for Correspondents "A" Through "K".   Uni-
        versity of Arkansas, 1965.

        A dissertation.   See: J. M. Moffett for
        "L" to "Z".

902   Peters, Robert Anthony
        A Study of Old English Words for Demon and
        Monster and Their Relation to English Place-
        Names.   University of Pennsylvania, 1961.

        A dissertation.

Petersen, Uwe
        See: 218.

Petre, J. E. Turville
    See: Turville-Petre, J. E.

903 Pfeiffer, Walter Mark
    The Cratylus: Plato's Investigation of Names.
    University of Toronto, 1971.

    A dissertation.

Phillips, James Orchard Halliwell
    See: Halliwell-Phillips, James Orchard

904 Philo-Shake (pseud.)
    "Orthography of Shakespeare's Name,"
    The Gentleman's Magazine, 57 (1787), 24-5.

905 Piel, Joseph M., and Dieter Kremer
    Hispano-gotisches Namenbuch. Heidelberg,
    Winter, 1976.

    A Hispano-Gothic book of names.

906 Pine, Leslie Gilbert
    The Story of Surnames. London, Country Life,
    1965.

    See also later editions.

    ---, See: 62.

907 Plank, R.
    "Names and Roles of Characters in Science
    Fiction", Names, 9 (1961), 151-9.

908 Ploss, Emil
    "Bamberg und die deutsche Literatur des 11. und
    12. Jahrhunderts," Jahrbuch für fränkische
    Landesforschung, 19 (1959), 275-302.

    On names in German heroic poetry from the Bambe
    region.

909 ---, "Die Nibelungenüberlieferung im Spiegel der
     langobardischen Namen," Forschungen und
     Fortschritte, 34 (1960), 53-60.

     On names in he Nibelungen.

910 Polányi, Michael, and Harry Prosch
     Meaning. University of Chicago Press, 1975.

     On names, see pp. 136-7: "Truth in Myths."

911 Polenz, Peter von
     "Name und Wort. Bermerkungen zur Metodik
     der Namendeutung," Mitteilungen für Namen-
     kunde, 8 (1960-1), 1-11.

     On name and word.

912 Politzer, Heinz
     Franz Kafka der Künstler. Frankfurt, Fischer,
     1965.

     On names; passim. See also English edition:
     Frank Kafka: Parable and Paradox. Ithaca,
     Cornell University Press, 1962.

913 Pollin, Alice M.
     The Gracioso of Significant Name in the
     Theater of Juan Ruiz de Alarcón y Mendoza.
     New York University, 1955.

     A dissertation.

914 ---, "Puns and Word Play in Calderon's Autos
     Sacramentales," Names, 16 (1968), 422-30.

915 Pollin, Burton R.
     "Byron, Poe, and Miss Matilda," Names, 16
     (1968), 390-414.

916 ---, Dictionary of Names and Titles in Poe's Col-
     lected Works. New York, Da Capo, 1968.

917 ---, "Names Used for Humor in Poe's Fiction," in
Love and Wrestling, Butch and O. K. Ed. by
Fred Tarpley. Commerce, Texas, Names Insti-
tute Press, 1973. (South Central Names
Institute Publication No. 2)

See pp. 51-7.

918 ---, Poe: Creator of Words. Baltimore, Enoch
Pratt Free Library, 1974.

919 ---, "Poe's Use of the Name Ermengarde in
Eleonora," Notes and Queries, 17 (1970),
332-3.

920 ---, "Poe's Use of the Name De Vere in "Lenore',"
Names, 23 (1975), 1-5.

921 ---, "Rappaccini's Daughter - Sources and Names,"
Names, 14 (1966), 30-5.

On names by Nathaniel Hawthorne.

922 Pommier, J.
"Noms et prénoms dans Madame Bovary,"
Mercure de France, 306 (1949), 244-64.

On names by Flaubert.

923 Porter, Mary Gray
A Dictionary of the Personal Names in the
Eddic Poems (Elder Edda and Eddica Minora).
University of North Carolina at Chapel Hill,
1960.

A dissertation.

924 Pott, August Friedrich
"Eigennamen in ihrem Unterschiede von Appel-
lativen und mit der Namengebung verbundener
Glaube und Sitte," Zeitschrift der morgen-
ländischen Gesellschaft, 24 (1870), 110-24.

The influence of first names on moral and
belief.

925 ---, Die Personennamen, insebesondere die Familiennamen und ihre Entstehungsarten. Unter
Berücksichtigung der Ortsnamen. Eine sprach-
liche Untersuchung. 2. Aufl. Reprint:
Wiesbaden, Sändig, 1968.

On the origin of personal and family names
with geographical considerations. Originally
published: Leipzig, Brochkhaus, 1859.

926 Potts, Cyrus Alvin
Dictionary of Bible Proper Names. Every
proper name in the Old and New Testament
arranged in alphabetical order; syllabified
and accented; vowel sound diacritically
marked; definitions given in Latin and
English. New York, Abingdon, 1922.

See also the revised and enlarged edition,
1923.

927 Power, M.
"Naming of Kathleen Kearney," Journal of
Modern Literature, 5 (1976), 532-4.

On the above name by James Joyce.

928 Power, William
"Middleton's Way with Names," Notes and
Queries, 205 (1960), 26-9, 56-60, 95-8,
136-40, and 175-9.

Pratt, Robert A.
See: 1147.

929 Preisigke, Friedrich
Namenbuch. Enthaltend alle griechischen,
lateinischen, ägyptischen, hebräischen,
arabischen und sonstigen semitischen und
nicht-semitischen Menschennamen, soweit sie
in griechischen Urkunden (Papyri, Ostraka,
Inschriften, Mumienschilden usw.) Ägyptens
sich vorfinden. Mit einem Anhang von Enno
Littmann, enthaltend die in diesem Namenbuch vorkommenden abessinischen, arabischen,
aramäischen, kanaanäischen und persischen
Namen. Heidelberg, 1922. Reprint: Amsterdam, Hakkert, 1967.

A book on Semitic and non-Semitic names.

---, See: 329.

930 Presber, Rudolf
     Ich gehe durch mein Haus. Erinnerungen.
     Stuttgart, Deutsche Verlagsanstalt, 1935.

     On an adventure with names in German litera-
     ture, see pp. 216-7. ("Erlebnisse mit
     Namen.")

     Pretzel, Ulrich
     See: 637.

931 "Proper Names in Poetry," Chambers's Edinburgh
     Journal, 6 (August 1846), 89-91.

932 Propper, Maximilian von
     "Zur Deutung eines Kryptogramms Goethes,"
     Goethe Jahrbuch, 92 (1975), 220-32.

     On a cryptogram by Goethe.

     Prosch, Harry
     See: 910.

933 Proust, Marcel
     "Names," in his On Art and Literature, 1896-
     1919. Tr. by Sylvia Towsend Warner. New York,
     Meridian, 1958.

     See pp. 230-47. See also original edition:
     Contre Sainte-Beuve; suivi de Nouveaux
     mélanges.

934 "Pseudonyms," Chambers's Journal, 6 (August 1856),
     65-7.

935 Puckett, Newbell Niles
     Black Names in America: Origins and Usages.
     Ed. by Murray Heller. Boston, Hall, 1975.

936 Pulgram, Ernst
        "Historisch-soziologische Betrachtung des
        modernen Familiennamens," Beiträge zur
        Namenforschung, 2 (1950-1), 132-65.

        On historical and sociological aspects of
        modern family names.

937 ---, "Name, Class Name, Noun," Die Sprache,
        5 (1959), 165-71.

938 ---, The Theory of Proper Names. Harvard Uni-
        versity, 1946.

        A dissertation.

939 ---, "Theory of Names," Beiträge zur Namenfor-
        schung, 5 (1954), 149-96.

     Pulling, Gyda
        See: 448.

940 "Pun Upon Names - More of It," Chambers's
        Journal, 22 (July 1854), 4-6.

941 Puntschoch, H.
        Die poetische Namengebung bei Stifter.
        Ebner-Eschenbach, Saar, Kürnberger, 1943.

        On Stifter's onomastics. A dissertation,
        Graz, 1943.

942 Quenon, Jean
       "Anthroponymie et caractérisation dans le
       théâtre de Max Frisch," Revue des Languages
       Vivantes - Tijdschrift voor Levende Talen,
       39 (1973), 526-37, and 40 (1974), 25-40.

       On names by Max Frisch.

943 Radzin, Hilda
      "The Discovery of 'Vinland' According to the
      Old Icelandic 'Eiriks Saga Rautha' and
      'Groenlendinga Thattr'," Literary Onomastics
      Studies, 2 (1975), 160-8.

944 ---, "The Names 'Gongu-Hrólf' in the Old Norse
      'Gongu-Hrólfs Saga'," Literary Onomastics
      Studies, 1 (1974), 47-52.

     Raine, Kathleen
          See: 714.

945 Rajec, Elizabeth M.
      "Kafkas Erzählung 'Blumfeld, ein älterer
      Junggeselle'. Ein onomastisch/interpreta-
      torischer Versuch," Beiträge zur Namen-
      forschung, 11 (1976), 464-9.

      On Kafka's names in the short story "Blumfeld,
      an Elderly Bachelor."

946 ---, Literarische Onomastik. Heidelberg, Winter,
      1977. (Beihefte der Beiträge zur Namenfor-
      schung, 12)

      A bibliography on German literary
      onomastics.

947 ---, Namen und ihre Bedeutungen im Werke Franz
      Kafkas. Ein interpretatorischer Versuch.
      Bern, Lang, 1977.

      On names in the works of Kafka. See also
      dissertation, City University of New York,
      1975.

948 Raper, P. E.
      Naamkunde-Bronnegids. Onomastics Source
      Guide, 1970. Tafelberg, Centre of Onomastic
      Sciences of the Human Sciences Research
      Council, 1972.

      A bibliography on South African onomastics;
      mainly on place-names.

949 Rasch, Gerhard
       Die bei den antiken Autoren überlieferten
       geographischen Namen im Raum nördlich der
       Alpen vom linken Rheinufer bis zur pannon-
       ischen Grenze; ihre Bedeutung und sprachliche
       Herkunft. 2 vols. Heidelberg, 1950.

       On toponyma in the works of classical authors.

950 Rat, Maurice
       "Mais non! Victor Hugo n'a pas inventé le
       fameux Jérimadeth," Figaro Littéraire, (Feb-
       ruary 7, 1948), 3.

       On a name by Hugo.

951 Rea, J.
       "Persephone in 'Corinna's Going A Maying',"
       College English, 26 (1965), 544-6.

       On names by Corinna.

    Read, William A.
       See: 507.

952 Reaney, Percy Hilde
       A Dictionary of British Surnames. 2nd ed.
       by R. M. Wilson. London, Routledge, 1976.

953 Reclams Namenbuch. Die wichtigsten deutschen
       und fremden Vornamen mit ihren Ableitungen
       und Bedeutungen. Hrsg. von Teo Herrle. 11.
       Aufl. Stuttgart, Reclam, 1973.

       A dictionary of names; general.

954 Reeves, Paschal
       "Thomas Wolfe's Old Catawba," Names, 11
       (1963), 254-6.

955 Reichenberger, A. G.
"A Review of 'Los nombres ₀..' by Morley-Tyler,"
Hispanic Review, 30 (1962), 160-2.

On names by Lope de Vega.

---, See: 802.

956 Reid, James Henderson
"Böll's Names," Modern Language Review, 69
(1974), 575-83.

957 Reisner, T. A.
"Blake's 'To Tirzah'," Explicator, 33
(1974), 3.

Reiss, Hans
See: 1310.

958 Rendall, Vernon
"The Names in Dickens," The New Statesman, 9
(September 1917), 614-5.

959 Renoir, A₀
"Chaucerian Character Names in Lydgate's
'Siege of Thebes'," Modern Languages Notes,
71 (1956), 249-56.

960 ---, "The Name Munsalvaesche in the 'Parzival'
of Wolfram von Eschenbach," Revue des
Langues Vivantes, 26 (1960), 470-1.

961 Reps, Saladin Paul
Exploring Our Name. A Psychological Tour
Through Names and Natures. Montrose, Pre-
view, 1938.

962 Reston, James
"What's in a Name?" The New York Times
(March 7, 1976), Section 4, 15.

An analysis of names in leading politicians.

963   Rhoden, B.
          "What's in a (Nick)name?" _Ebony_, 31 (May
          1976), 70-2.

964   Richards Ivor Armstrong
          Principles of Literary Criticism. New York
          Harcourt, 1925.

          See pp. 147-8 on names in literature. See
          also the later edition.

965   Richardson, Peter N.
          German-Romance Contact: Name-Giving in
          Walser Settlements. Amsterdam, Rodopi, 1974.
          (Amsterdamer Publicationen zur Sprache und
          Literatur, 15)

      ---, See: 1106.

966   Richardt, Rosemarie
          "Bibliographie zur russischen Namenforschung
          mit Beiträgen von M. Vasmer und B. O.
          Unbegaun," _Onoma_, 5 (1955-6), 1-76.

          A bibliography on Russian onomastics.

967   Richmond, Winthrop E.
          "Ballad Place Names," _Journal of American_
          Folklore, 59 (1946), 263-7.

968   ---, _Place Names in the English and Scottish_
          Popular Ballads and Their American Variants.
          Ohio State University, 1947.

          A dissertation.

969   Richter, W.
          "Beiträge zur Deutung des Mittelteils des
          Nibelungenliedes I. Der Name Nibelunge,"
          Zeitschrift für deutsches Altertum und
          deutsche Literatur, 72 (1935), 9-16.

          On the name "Nibelunge."

970 Riehl, Robert Ellison
     The Ordeal of Naming: Walker Percy's Philo-
     sophy of Language and His Novels. University
     of Texas at Austin, 1975.

     A dissertation.

     Riesner, Dieter
        See: 372.

971 Ristic, O.
     "Leksičko-semantičke odlike tvorbe imenica
     u nekih srpskih i hrvatskih romantičarskih
     pesnika," Južnoslovenski filolog, 28 (1969),
     220-320.

     On names in Serbian and in Croatian romantic
     songs.

972 Ritter, Otto
     "Lauthistorisches zum Namen Don Andriano de
     Armado," in Probleme der englischen Sprache
     und Kultur₀ Festschrift Johannes Hoops zum
     60. Geburtstag. Hrsg. von Wolfgang Keller.
     Heidelberg, Winter, 1925.

     On Don Adriano de Armado's name.

973 Rizvi, Maulana S. S. A.
     "'Zenj': Its First Known Use in Arabic
     Literature," Azania (Nairobi), 2 (1967),
     200-1.

     On the use of the above name in a seventh-
     century Arabic poem.

974 Roberts, Ruth Eloise
     Welsh Place Names in the Earliest Arthurian
     Texts. Columbia University, 1957.

     A dissertation.

     Robertson, J. M.
        See: 414.

     Robert-Tornow, Walter
        See: 1.

975   Robinson, Fred C.
          "Appropriate Naming in English Literature,"
          Names, 20 (1972), 131-7.

976   ---, "Personal Names in Medieval Narrative and
          the Name of Unferth in Beowulf," in Essays
          in Honor of Richebourg Gaillard McWilliams.
          Ed. by Howard Creed. Birmingham, 1970.

          See pp. 43-8.

977   ---, "The Significance of Names in Old English
          Literature," Anglia, 86 (1968), 14-58.

978   ---, "Some Uses of Name-Meanings in Old English
          Poetry," Neuphilologische Mitteilungen, 69
          (1968), 161-71.

979   Robinson, R.
          "Criticism of Plato's Cratylus," Philosophi-
          cal Review, 65 (1956), 324-41.

980   Robinson, Walter Langridge
          Name Charactrerization in the Works of Thomas
          Mann. University of Texas at Austin, 1959.

          A dissertation.

981   Rochetal, A. de
          Le Caractère par le prénom. Paris, Bischoff,
          1907. (Une science nouvelle: L'onomatologie)

          On the character of first names.

982   Rodale, Jerome Irving
          The Phrase Finder, Name-Word Finder, Metaphor
          Finder, Sophisticated Synonyms. Compiled by
          J. I. Rodale with the collaboration of Edward
          J. Fluck. Emmaus, Rodale, 1958.

983   Roe, Frank Gordon
          "Surnames in Dickens," The Dickensian, 31
          (March 1935), 83-90.

984   Roelandts, K., and P. J. Meertens
       Nederlandse Familiennamen in historisch
       perspectief. Leuven, Institut voor Naam-
       kunde, 1951. (Anthroponymica, 4 Onomastica
       Nederlandica)

       On family names on the Netherlands.

985   Rogers, P. Burwell
       "The Names of the Canterbury Pilgrims,"
       Names, 16 (1968), 339-46.

       On names by Chaucer.

986   Rojas, Victor J.
       "Onomastics and the Prismatic Reality in the
       Poetry of Fernando Pessoa," Literary Onomas-
       tics Studies, 4 (1977), 97-104.

987   Rolfe, William James
       A Life of William Shakespeare. Boston,
       Estes, 1904.

       On Shakespeare's name, see pp. 17-24.

988   Rölleke, Heinz
       "Kann man das Wesen gewöhnlich aus dem Namen
       lesen? Zur Deutung der Namen in der Juden-
       buche der Annette von Droste-Hülshoff,"
       Euphorion, 70 (1976), 409-14.

       On Annette von Droste-Hülshoff's names.

989   Rollman, Wilfred J.
       "Artistry of Gide's Onomastics," Modern
       Language Notes, 86 (1971), 523-31.

       ---, See: 888.

990   Romanoff, Paul
       Onomasticon of Palestine. A new method in
       post Biblical topography. New York, (n. p.)
       1937.

       On geographical names.

991 Rooth, Erik
     "Zur Forschungslage in betreff des
     Namens Ludwig," Beiträge zur Namenforschung,
     6 (1971), 207-14.

     On the name "Ludwig."

     Rosenberg, Bruce A.
     See: 820.

992 Rosenfeld, Hellmut
     "Die Kosenamen und Lockrufe unserer Haus-
     tiere und die Leitrufe unserer Zugtiere,"
     Rheinisches Jahrbuch für Volkskunde, 6
     (1956), 50-90.

     On the names of animals.

993 ---, "Die Magie des Namens. Bayerische Tierkose-
     namen als volkstümliche Sprachschöpfung,"
     Bayerisches Jahrbuch für Volkskunde (1950),
     94-8.

     On the magic of animal names.

994 ---, "Der Name des Dichters Ulrich Fuetrer und
     die Orthographie insbesondere die Zwielaut-
     und Umlautbezeichnumg in bairischen Hand-
     schriften des 15. Jahrhunderts," Studia
     Neophilologica, 37 (1965), 166-233.

     On Ulrich Fuetrer's name.

995 ---, "Der Name Wieland," Beiträge zur Namenfor-
     schung, 4 (1969), 53-62.

     On names in German heroic literature.

996 ---, "Die Namen der Heldendichtung, insbesondere
     Nibelung, Hagen, Wate, Hetel, Horand, Gudrun,"
     Beiträge zur Namenforschung, 1 (1966), 231-65.

     On names in German heroic literature.

997 ---, Personen-, Orts- und Ländernamen in Wolframs Parzival," in Studien zur Namenkunde und Sprachgeographie. Festschrift für Karl Finsterwalder zum 70. Geburtstag. Hrsg. von Wolfgang Meid, Hermann M. Ölberg, Hans Schmeja. Innsbruck, Institut für Vergleichende Sprachwissenschaft der Universität, 1971. (Innsbrucker Beiträge zur Kulturwissenschaft, Bd. 16)

On personal names and toponyma in Wolfram's "Parzival," see pp. 203-14.

998 ---, "Vorzeitnamen und Gegenwartsnamen in der mittelalterlichen Dichtung und die Schichtung der Namen," 10. Internationaler Kongress für Namenforschung, Wien, Verlag der Wiener Medizinieschen Akademie, 1969.

On names in literature of the Middle Ages see 10/2, pp. 333-40.

---, See: 461.

999 Round, John Horace
"English Surnames," The Quarterly Review, 180 (January 1895), 207-30.

A collection of reviews on surnames.

1000 Rozenberg-Sacks, Hélène
"Allegory and Nominal Identity in Melville's Poem 'Clarel'," Literary Onomastics Studies, 1 (1974), 40-6.

Ruberg, Uwe:
See: 454.

1001 Ruberg, V.
"A Review of G. D. West's 'An Index to Proper ...'," Beiträge zur Namenforschung, 6 (1971), 174-5.

On proper names in French Arthurian verse.

---, See: 1292.

1002 Rudman, Harry W.
    "A Possible Prototype of Mann's Settembrini,"
    The Germanic Review, 25 (1950), 299.

1003 Rudnyts'kyi, J. B.
    "Functions of Proper Names in Literary Work,"
    in Stil- und Formprobleme in der Literatur.
    Hrsg. von Paul Böckmann. Heidelberg, Winter,
    1959.

    See pp. 378-83.

1004 ---, "Svjatogor - the Name of the Hero of Bylina,"
    Names, 10 (1962), 229-32.

    On the above name in the Russian legend.

1005 Rudwin, Maximilian Josef
    "The Name of the Devil," in his "The Devil
    in Legend and Literature. Chicago, Open
    Court, 1931.

    See pp. 26-34.

1006 Rudzitis, J.
    "Daugavas vilnu cikls Kārla Skalbes dzejā,"
    Cela zimes (London), 47 (1971), 282-9.

    On names in the poetry of Kārlis Skalbe.

1007 Ruello, Francis
    Les 'Noms divins' et leurs 'raisons' selon
    Saint Albert le Grand, commentateur de
    'De divine nominibus'. Université de Paris,
    1963.

    A dissertation on Albertus Magnus, Saint.
    See also the other edition: Paris, Vrin,
    1963.

1008 Ruffner, James A.
    Eponyms Dictionaries Index. Ed. by James A.
    Ruffner. Associate editors: Jennifer Berger
    and Georgia Schoenung. Detroit, Gale, 1977.

    Includes eponyms drawn from literature.

1009 Ruggieri, R. M.
"Su alcune incarnacioni demoniachi nella
letteratura gallaromanza e romena," Actele
celui de al XII-lea Congres International
de Linguistica si Filologie Romanica,
Bucarest, Edit. Acad. Rep. Soc. Romania,
1970-1.

On literary onomastics. See: 12/1, pp.
1129-36.

Rüke-Dravina, Velta
See: 363.

1010 Rule, Lareina, and William K. Hammond
What's in a Name? Surnames in America.
New York, Pyramid, 1973.

See also the later edition.

1011 Rümmele, Doris
Mikrokosmos im Wort. Zur Ästhetik der
Namengebung bei Thomas Mann. Freiburg
Universität, 1968.

A dissertation on the names used by Thomas
Mann.

1012 Rusell, Harris L.
The Appropriate Name of the Metamorphoses
of Apuleius. University of Illinois at
Urbana Champaign, 1943.

A dissertation.

1013 Ruttner, Eckhard
"The Names in Solzhenitsyn's Short Novel:
One Day in the Life of Ivan Denisovich,"
Names, 23 (1975), 103-11.

Ryan, John
See: 333.

1014 Ryan, J. S.
Language in the Aboriginal Novel. London,
Goodwin, 1970.

Refers to proper names in Australian literature, passim on names.

Sachs, Hélène Rozenberg
    See: Rozenberg-Sachs, Hélène

1015 Sadler, F.
    "Crane's Fleming: Appellation for Coward or
    Hero?" American Literature, 48 (1976), 372-6.

1016 Saillens, E.
    "Du nom propre en littérature," Mercure de
    France, 268 (1936), 268-9.

    On proper names in French literature.

1017 Saintsbury, George
    "Names in Fiction," Macmillan's Magazine, 59
    (December 1888), 115-20.

1018 Salimova, R. H.
    "Nekotorye nabljudenija nad antroponimiej russ-
    kich bylin (v zapiskach XVII-XVIII v.)," in
    Samarkandskij Universitet im. A. Navoi.
    Naučnoteoret. konferencija profess. Samarkand,
    1969.

    See pp. 38-42 on personal names in Russian
    legends.

1019 ---, "Nekotorye voprosy strukturoobrazovanija imen
    sobstvennych bylinnogo eposa v sopostavlenii
    s appeljativnym slovarnym sostavom russkogo
    jazyka," in Jazyk i literatura , Samarkand,
    1969.

    See pp. 139-46 on the structure of proper
    names in the Russian epos and in the Russian
    language.

    Salis, Renzo Sertoli
        See: Sertoli Salis, Renzo

1020 San-Marte
    "Wer ist San Ze?" Beiträge zur Geschichte
    der deutschen Sprache und Literatur, 9 (1884),
    145-6.

    On above name in Gottfried von Strassburg's
    Tristan.

1021 Sargent, B. N.
"Frise: le nom et le lieu dans la littérature en ancien et moyen français," in Festschrift W. J. Buma. Grins, Wolters, 1970.

On names in Old and Middle French literature,
see pp. 18-24.

1022 Satin, Joseph
"The Symbolic Role of Cordelia in King Lear,"
Forum, 9 (Fall-Winter 1972), 15-7.

On the above name by Shakespeare.

1023 Sayers, W.
"Rummaret de Wenelande: A Geographical Note
to Wace's Brut," Romance Philology, 18 (1964),
46-53.

Scanff, Jacques Le
See: Le Scanff, Jacques

1024 Schäfer, Hans-Wilhelm
"Die Planetennamen in Wolframs Parzival,"
Zeitschrift für deutsche Sprache, 21 (1965),
60-8.

On the names of planets in "Parzival."

1025 Schaller, D.
"A Review of D. C. Swanson's 'The Names in
Roman Verse ...'," Beiträge zur Namenforschung,
4 (1969), 85-6.

---, See: 1182.

1026 Schauer, Erika
Die Personen- und Ortsnamen in Gottfried von
Strassburgs 'Tristan und Isolt' nach metrischen
Gesichtspunkten. Wien, 1950.

A dissertation on personal and geographical
names in the "Tristan and Isolt" by Gottfried
von Strassburg.

1027 Scherer, A.
       "Zum Sinngehalt der germanischen Personennamen,"
       Beiträge zur Namenforschung, 4 (1953), 1-37.

       On Germanic pesonal names.

1028 Schibanoff, S.
       "Argus and Argyve: Etymology and Character-
       ization in Chaucer's Troilus," Speculum, 51
       (1976), 647-58.

1029 Schiffmann, K.
       "Heldensage und Namengebung," Zeitschrift für
       österreichischen Gymnasien, 54 (1903), 193-200.

       On names in German heroic literature.

     Schirmer, Karl-Heinz
       See: 616.

1030 Schlaffer, H.
       "Namen und Buchstaben in Goethes 'Wahlver-
       wandtschaften'," Jahrbuch der Jean-Paul-
       Gesellschaft, 7 (1972), 84-102.

       On names by Goethe.

1031 Schlaug, Wilhelm
       Die altsächsischen Personennamen vor dem
       Jahre 1000. Lund, 1962. (Lunder germa-
       nistische Forschungen, 34)

       On Old Sachsonian personal names.

1032 ---, Studien zu den altsächsischen Personennamen
       des 11. und 12. Jahrhunderts. Lund, 1955.
       (Lunder germanistische Forschungen, 30)

       On Old Sachsonian personal names from the
       eleventh and twelfth centuries, see pp. 20-2.

     Schmeja, Hans
       See: 609, 997, 1175.

1033 Schmidt, Johanna
"Der Namenschatz in Tacitus' Germania,"
Beiträge zur Namenforschung, 5 (1954), 269-
71.

On the sentence name in Tacitus' "Germania."

1034 Schmitt, Rüdiger
Indogermanische Dichtersprache und Namengebung. Vortrag. Innsbruck, Institute für
Sprachwissenschaft der Universität Innsbruck,
1973. (Innsbrucker Beiträge zur Sprachwissenschaft, Vorträge, 10)

On Indo-Germanic personal names.

Schmitz, L. Dora
See: 285, 286.

1035 Schneider, Karl
Die germanischen Runennamen. Versuch einer
Gesamtdeutung. Ein Beitrag zur ind./germ.
Kultur- und Religionsgeschichte. Meisenheim,
Hain, 1956.

A dissertation on Germanic names.

---, See: 731.

Schoenung, Goergia
See: 1008.

1036 Scholl, Emma
Die flexivische Behandlung der fremden Eigennamen in den althochdeutschen und altsächsischen Denkmälern. Zürich, 1906.

On the influence of foreign names in Old High
German and Old Sachsonian sources.

037 Schönfeld, Moritz
Wörterbuch der altgermanischen Personen- und Völkernamen. Nach der Überlieferung des klassischen Altertums. Heidelberg, Winter, 1911. Reprint: 2nd ed. 1965. (Germanische Bibliothek. Sammlung germanischer Elementar- und Handbücher, Wörterbücher, Bd. 2)

Based on his dissertation, Groningen, 1906: Proeve eener kritische verzameling van Germaansche volks- en persoonsnamen. A dictionary of Old Germanic personal names.

038 Schoolfield, G. C.
"Hagar Olsson's Chitambo: Anniversary Thoughts on Names and Structure," Scandinavian Studies, 45 (1973), 223-62.

Schotch, P. K.
See: 740.

039 Schramm, Gottfried
"Eine hunnisch-germanische Namenbezeichnung?" Jahrbuch für fränkische Landesforschung, 20 (1960), 129-55.

On Hun-Germanic names in heroic poetry.

040 ---, "Etzels Vater Botelung," Beiträge zur Namenforschung, 1 (1966), 266-90.

On the name "Botelung."

041 ---, "Der Name Kriemhilt," Zeitschrift für deutsches Altertum und deutsche Literatur, 94 (1965), 39-57.

On the name "Kriemhilt."

042 ---, Namenschatz und Dichtersprache. Studien zu den zweigliedrigen Personennamen der Germanen. Göttingen, Vandenhoeck, 1957. (Ergänzungshefte zur Zeitschrift für vergleichende Sprachforschung aug dem Gebiet der indogermanischen Sprachen, Nr. 15)

On German personal names.

-173-

———, See: 7.

1043 Schreiber, R.
"Vornamen als Quellen volkskundlicher Forschung," Sudetendeutche Zeitschrift für Volkskunde, 1 (1932), 142-56.

On names as sources of folklore research.

1044 Schröder, Edward
"Blattsfüllsel. Ein Zeugnis zur Wielandsage,"
Zeitschrift für deutsches Altertum und deutsche
Literatur, 45 (1920), 143-4.

On names in the Wielandsaga.

1045 ———, Deutsche Namenkunde. Gesammelte Aufsätze zur
Kunde deutscher Personen- und Ortsnamen.
Festgabe seiner Freunde und Schüler zum 80.
Geburtstag. Göttingen, Vandenhoeck, 1938.

Essays on German onomastics. See also the
1944 edition by Ludwig Wolff.

1046 ———, "Wieland der Schmied. Ein Exkurs über Personennamen aus der Heldensage," Zeitschrift für
deutsches Altertum und deutsche Literatur, 53
(1912), 329-35.

On onomastics in German heroic literature.

1047 ———, "Zufälligkeit in Eigennamen," in Festschrift
Max H. Jellinek zum 29. Mai 1928 dargebracht.
Wien, Österreichischer Bundesverlag für Unter-
richt, Wissenschaft und Kunst, 1928.

On the peculiarities of first names, see pp.
105-11.

1048 Schumacher, Heinz
Lobgesange biblischer Namen. Zusammengestellt
nach den biblischen Eigennamen in I. Chron. 1-9,
die mit den Gottesnamen El-Elohim oder Jah-Jahwe/
Jehova zusammengesetzt sind. Mit wörtlicher und
in Form von Psalmen umschreibender Übersetzung.
Stuttgart, Paulus, 1964.

On Biblical names.

1049 ---, Die Namen der Bibel und ihr Bedeutung in
Deutschen. Nach Deutungen von Th. Burgstahler
und Georg Kahn, und unter Vergleich von
Wörterbüchern, Konkordanzen und älteren
Namenbüchern zusammengestellt. Stuttgart,
Paulus, 1958.

On Biblical names.

1050 Schumacher, Theo
"Riuwental," Beiträge zur Namenforschung, 11
(1960), 91-5.

On the name "Neidhart."

1051 Schützeichel, Rudolf
"A Reply to Coseriu's 'Sprachtheorie ...',"
Beiträge zur Namenforschung, 11 (1976), 238.

On theory of proper names.

---, See: 218.

1052 ---, "Historische Treue bei historischer Wort-
und Namenforschung," in Festschrift für Karl
Bischoff zum 70. Geburtstag. Hrsg. von Günter
Bellmann, Günter Eifler, Wolfgang Kleiber.
Köln, Böhlau, 1975.

On historical accuracy of onomastics.

1053 ---, "Die Kölner Namenliste des Londoner Ms. Harley
2805. Mit einem Faksimile," in Namenforschung.
Festschrfit für Adolf Bach zum 75. Geburtstag
am 31. Januar 1965. Hrsg. von Rudolf
Schützeichel und Matthias Zender. Heidelberg,
Winter, 1968.

See pp. 97-126. On the influence of names on
German heroic literature, see p. 125.

1054 ---, "Register der 'Beiträge zur Namenforschung,
Bd. 1-16'," in Verbindung mit Ernst Dickenmann und Jürgen Untermann. Heidelberg, Winter,
1969.

An index to vols. 1-16 of Beiträge zur Namenforschung. Includes references to literary
onomastics.

1055 ---, "Zu Adolf Socins oberrheinischem Namenbuch,"
Beiträge zur Namenforschung, 4 (1969), 1-52.

On Socin's book of German names, see pp. 37
and 41.

---, See: 1118.

1056 ---, "Zum Hildebrandslied," in Typologia litterarum.
Festschrift für Max Wehrli. Hrsg. von Stefan
Sonderegger, Alois M. Haas, Harald Burger. Zürich,
Atlantis, 1969.

See pp. 83-94 on names in the "Hildebrandlied."

---, See: 132, 401, 761, 823.

1057 Schwake, H. P.
"Zur Frage der Namenssymbolik im höfischen
Roman," Germanisch-romanische Monatsschrift,
20 (1970), 338-53.

On name symbolism in courtly novels.

1058 Schwartz, Stephen P.
Naming, Necessity, and Natural Kinds. Ithaca,
Cornell University Press, 1977.

1059 ---, "The Use of Onomastics in Germanic Linguistics. The First Steps," Names, 16 (1968),
119-26.

Original title: "Typological and Genetic
Classification of the Germanic Language as
Reflected in the Earliest German Names."

1060 Schwarz, Ernst
Deutsche Namenforschung. 2 vols. Göttingen,
Vandenhoeck, 1949-50.

On German onomastics.

1061 ---, Sudetendeutsche Familiennamen aus vorhussitischer
Zeit. Köln, Böhlau, 1957. (Ostmitteleuropa in
Vergangenheit und Gegenwart, 3)

On German literary onomastics, see pp. 14 and 25-6.

1062 Scott, F. R.
        "Lady Honoria Howard and the Name of the
        Chief Female Character in 'The Rival Ladies',"
        Review of English Studies, 20 (1944), 158-9.

        On names by John Dryden.

1063 Scott, John A.
        "Patronymics as a Test of the Relative Age of
        Homeric Books," Classical Philology, 7 (1912),
        293-301.

1064 Scoufos, A. L.
        "Harvey: A Name-Change in Henry IV," English
        Literary History, 36 (1969), 297-318.

        On names by Shakespeare.

1065 Seaman, William M.
        The Appropriate Name in Plautus. University
        of Illinois at Urbana Champaign, 1939.

        A dissertation.

1066 ---, "On the Names of Old and Young Men in Plautus,"
        Illinois University Studies in Language and
        Literature, 58 (1969), 114-22.

1067 ---, "The Roman Name in Historical Fiction," The
        Classical Journal, 51 (1955), 27-31.

1068 ---, "The Understanding of Greek by Plalutus'
        Audience," The Classical Journal, 50 (1954),
        115-9.

1069 Searle, William G.
        Onomasticon Anglo-Saxonicum. Cambridge, 1897.
        Reprint: New York, Olms, 1969.

1070 Sébillot, Paul Yves
        "Les personnages dan les proverbs," Revue des
        Traditions Populaires, 18 (1903), 172-6.

        On names in proverbs.

1071 Seidel, Michael
　　　Epic Geography:　James Joyce's 'Ulysses'.
　　　Maps by Thomas Crawford.　Princeton Univer-
　　　sity Press, 1976.

1072 Selby, Robert H.
　　　"The Italian Names in Ben Jonson's 'Every Man
　　　Out of His Humour'," in Of Edsels and Marauders
　　　Ed. by F. Tarpley and A. Moseley.　Commerce,
　　　Texas, Names Institute Press, 1971.　(South
　　　Central Names Institute Publication No. 1)

　　　See pp. 97-106.

1073 Sélten, Bo
　　　Early East-Anglican Nicknames, 'Shakespeare
　　　Names'.　Lund, CWK Gleerup, 1969.

　　　The above names listed in alphabetical order.

1074 ---, The Anglo-Saxon Heritage in Middle-English
　　　Personal Names.　Lund, Gleerup, 1972.　(Lund
　　　Studies in English, Vol. 43)

1075 Sennewald, Charlotte
　　　Die Namengebung bei Dickens.　Eine Studie über
　　　Lautsymbolik.　Leipzig, Mayer, 1936.　(Palaestr
　　　203.　Untersuchungen und Texte aus der deutsche
　　　und englischen Philologie)

　　　A dissertation on names by Dickens.

1076 Seronsky, Cecil C.
　　　"Some Proper Names in 'Gulliver's Travels',"
　　　Notes and Queries, 202 (1957), 470-1.

　　　On names by Swift.

1077 Sertoli Salis, Renzo
　　　Dizionario dei nomi propri di persona.　Milano,
　　　Ceschina, 1951.

　　　A dictionary of Italian proper names.

1078 Sewell, Ernestine
        "Name-Calling in English Literature," in Love
        and Wrestling, Butch and O.K. Ed. by F. Tarpley.
        Commerce, Texas, Names Institute Press, 1973.
        (South Central Names Institute Publication No.
        2)

        See pp. 58-64.

1079 Shaaber, M. A.
        "Shylock's Name," Notes and Queries, 195 (1950),
        236.

        On the above name by Shakespeare.

     Shak Miso
        See: Miso-Shak (pseud.)

1080 "Shakespeare - and Readers," The Rotarian, 55
        August 1939), 4.

1081 "Shakespeare's Name," The Eclectic Magazine, 13
        (1848), 431.

1082 "Shakespeare's Name," The Rotarian, 49 (July
        1936), 24-6.

        See also Readers Digest, 29 (August 1936),
        95-8 under title: "My Name Is William
        Shakespeare."

1083 Shankland, H.
        "Dante Aliger," Modern Language Review, 70
        (1975), 764-85.

1084 Shankle, George Earlie
        American Nicknames. Their Origin and Signifi-
        cance. New York, Wilson, 1955.

1085 Shawcross, John T.
        "The Etymological Significance of Biblical
        Names in 'Paradise Regain'd'," Literary
        Onomastics Studies, 2 (1975), 34-57.

        On names by Milton.

1086 Sherbo, A.
        "Fielding's Dogs," _Notes and Queries_, 17
        (1970), 302-3.

1087 Shipley, Joseph T.
        Dictionary of Word Origins. New York, Philo-
        sophical Library, 1945. Reprint: Ames, 1955.

1088 Shirt, David J.
        "A Note on the Etymology of 'Le Morholt',"
        Tristania, 1 (1975), 21-8.

1089 Sibbald, K. M.
        "An Onomastic Calendar of Saints in Lorca's
        Romancero Gitano," _Literary Onomastics Studies_,
        3 (1976), 56-78.

1090 Siebs, Benno Eide
        Die Personennamen der Germanen. Wiesbaden,
        Sändig, 1970.

        On Germanic personal names.

1091 Siegchrist, M.
        "Pollyana or Polyanthus: Clara de Millefleurs
        in Browning's Red Cotton Night-Cap Country
        (Temptresses)," _English Language Notes_, 11
        (1974), 283-7.

     Sievers, Edward
        See: 880.

1092 Silverman, Michael Henry
        _Jewish Personal Names in the Elephantine
        Documents: A Study in Onomastic Development_,
        Brandeis Unniversity, 1967.

        A dissertation.

1093 Sims, Eleanor G.
        _The Garrett Manuscript of the Zafar-Name: A
        Study in Fifteenth-Century Timurid Patronage_.
        New York, New York University, 1973.

        A dissertation.

1094 Singerman, Robert
Jewish and Hebrew Onomastics. A Bibliography.
New York, Garland, 1977.

Singleton, Charles S.
See: 1224.

1095 Sipahigil, T.
"Othello's Name Once Again," Notes and Queries,
18 (1971), 147-8.

On the above name by Shakespeare.

1096 Skornjakova, M. F.
"Ob upotreblenii imen sobstvennych v reči,"
Učen. zap. Sverdlovsk, 1969.

On the usage of proper names in the Russian
language: also on names by Gorkij, see pp.
54-60.

1097 Skorobohata, E.
"Proper Names of Greek Origin in Ovid's Metamorphoses," Onomastica (Winnipeg), 32 (1966).

1098 Skutil, J.
"Mistni, pomistni a osobni jména v Mrštikovém
'Roku na vsi'. (Na okraj otázky onomastika v
literárnim dile), in Od Hradské cesty, 1968-9.

See pp. 93-5 on place-names, minor place-names
and personal names in the Czech novel "A Year
in the Village" by V. A. Mrštik.

Šlajsová, M. Nováková
See: Nováková-Šlajsová, M.

1099 Slavick, William H.
"Ellison's Nameless," in They Had to Call It
Something. Ed. by F. Tarpley. Commerce, Texas,
Names Institute Press, 1974. (South Central
Names Institute Publication No. 3)

See pp. 119-24.

Slote, Bernice
        See: 815.

1100 Smelser, Marshall
        "Poets and Place Names," <u>Names</u>, 1 (1953),
        15-9.

1101 Šmilauer, V.
        "A Review of U. Halfmann's 'Zur Symbolik der
        Personennamen ...'," <u>Zpravodaj Místopisné
        Komise Československé Akademie Věd</u>, 11 (1970),
        109-10.

        On O'Neill's names.

        ---, See: 432.

1102 ---, "Jméno Tandariáš," <u>Zpravodaj Místopisné
        Komise Československé Akademie Věd</u>, 11 (1970),
        676-7.

        On the name "Tandariáš" in an old Czech folklore

1103 Smith, Benjamin E.
        See: 171, 172.

1104 Smith, Elsdon C.
        <u>American Surnames</u>. Philadelphia, Chilton, 1969.

1105 ---, "A Review of G. D. West's 'An Index of Proper
        Names in French Arthurian Verse Romances 1150-
        1300'," <u>Names</u>, 18 (1970), 311.

        ---, See: 1292.

1106 ---, "A Review of P. N. Richardson's 'German-
        Romance Contact: Name-Giving in Walser Settle-
        ments'," <u>Names</u>, 23 (1975), 301-3.

        ---, See: 965.

1107 ---, Bibliography on Personal Names," <u>Names</u>, 1
(1953-   ).

Includes bibliographical entries on literary
onomastics. Up-dated on a yearly basis.

1108 ---, "Books in English on Personal Names," <u>Names</u>,
1 (1953), 197-202.

1109 ---, <u>Dictionary of American Family Names</u>. New
York, Harper, 1956.

1110 ---, <u>New Dictionary of American Names</u>. New York,
Harper, 1973.

Originally published under title: <u>Dictionary
of American Family Names</u>.

1111 ---, <u>Personal Names, A Bibliography</u>. New York, New
York Public Library, 1952.

See pp. 100-3 on "Names in Literature."

---, See: 13, 1107.

1112 ---, "Popular Names," <u>The American Magazine</u>, 137
(June 1944), 8.

1113 ---, <u>The Story of Our Names</u>. Detroit, Gale,
1970.

1114 Smith, Laura
"Charactonyms in the Fiction of Nathaniel
Hawthorne," in <u>Of Edsels and Marauders</u>, Ed.
by F. Tarpley and A. Moseley. Commerce,
Texas, Names Institute Press, 1971. (South
Central Names Institute Publication No. 1)

See pp. 75-81.

1115 ---, "Fictive Names in Mark Twain's 'Pudd'nhead
Wilson'," in <u>Love and Wrestling, Butch and O.K.</u>
Ed. by F. Tarpley. Commerce, Texas, Names In-
stitute Press, 1973. (South Central Names
Institute Publication No. 2)

See. pp. 91-4.

1116 Smith, Roland M.
"Irish Names in 'The Faerie Queene',"
Modern Language Notes, 61 (1946), 27-38.

On names by E. Spenser.

1117 ---, "Swift's Little Language and Nonsense Names,"
Journal of English and Germanic Philology,
53 (1954), 178-96.

---, See: 194.

1118 Socin, Adolf
Mittelhochdeutsches Namenbuch nach oberrhei-
nischen Quellen des 12. und 13. Jahrhunderts.
Basel, Helbing, 1903. Reprint: 1966.

On Middle High German names in heroic literature, see pp. 565-73.

---, See: 1055.

1119 Solmsen, Felix
Indogermanische Eigennamen als Spiegel der
Kulturgeschichte. Hrsg. von Ernst Fraenkel.
Heidelberg, Fraenkel, 1922. (Indogermanische
Bibliothek, IV, 2)

1120 Solov'eva, A. K.
"Materialy dlja izučenija prozvišč po perepiske
K. Marksa i F. Engelsa," Antroponimika (1970),
166-79.

On names in the works of Marx and Engels.

Sonderegger, Stefan.
See: 1056.

1121 Sonnenfeld, Marion
"An Etymological Explanation of the Hagen
Figure," Neophilologus, 43 (1959), 300-4.

On the above name in Germanic heroic
literature.

1122 ---, "The Origin of Hagen," Literary Onomastics Studies, 3 (1976), 79-93.

1123 Sorensen, Holger Steen
The Meaning of Proper Names, with a Definiens Formula for Proper Names in Modern English. Copenhagen, G.E.C. Gad, 1963.

1124 Sorgenfrei, G.
"Personennamen in Titeln literarischer Werke," Sprachpflege, 19 (1970), 52-6.

On personal names in the titles of literary works.

Sothern, E. H.
See: 530.

1125 Sotiroff, G.
"Homeric Overtones in Contemporary Macedonian Toponymy," Onomastica (Quebec), 41 (1971).

1126 ---, "Names of Four Emperors in the Book of Giacomo di Pietro Luccari," Names, 20 (1972), 188-228.

1127 ---, "Slavonic Names in Greek and Roman Antiquities," Onomastica (Quebec), 37 (1969).

1128 Soudek, Ernst
Meister Eckhart. Stuttgart, Metzler, 1973. (Sammlung Metzler, 120)

On the name "Eckhart," see p. 16.

Sowinski, Bernhardt
See: 616.

1129 Spitzer, L.
"Études d'anthroponymie ancienne française; Olivier de la Chanson de Roland," Publications of the Modern Language Association, 58 (1943), 589-93.

On names in the "Chanson de Roland."

1130 ---, "Name of Roland's Sword," Language, 15 (1939), 48-50.

1131 Splett, Jochen
Rüdiger von Bechelaren. Studien zum zweiten
Teil des Nibelungenliedes. Heidelberg, Winter,
1968. (Germanische Bibliothek, Untersuchungen
und Einzeldarstellungen)

On names in German medieval literature, see
pp. 25-43. See also dissertation, Bonn.

1132 Stafford, William T.
Name, Title and Place Index to the Critical
Writings of Henry James. Englewood, IHS
Library, 1975.

Originally published under title: Index to
Henry James: Criticism and Essays.

1133 Stanford, W. B.
"New Name for Ulysses' Daughter?" Classical
Review, 23 (1973), 126.

On the above name in the post-Homeric tradition.

Stang, Christian S.
See: 363.

1134 Stanley, E. G.
"Richard Hyrd (?) 'rote of resoun ryht' in ms
Harley 2253," Notes and Queries, 22 (1975),
155-7.

On Middle English names.

1135 Stansfield, Martha
The Use of Personal Names in Roman Satire.
University of Chicago, 1932.

A dissertation.

1136 Stark, Franz
Keltische Forschungen. 2 vols. Wien, Gerold, 1869.

On Celtic names from the seventh to the tenth centuries, see Vol. 2: "Keltische Personennamen nachgewiesen in den Ortsbenennungen des Codex traditionum ecclesiac Ravennatensis aus dem 7-10. Jahrhundert."

1137 ---, Die Kosenamen der Germanen. Eine Studie, Wien, Tendler, 1868.

On Germanic names.

1138 Stark, Jurgen Kurt
Personal Names in Palmyrene Inscriptions. Oxford, Clarendon, 1971.

See also dissertation: Johns Hopkins University, 1968.

1139 Staton, W. F.
"A Reply to H. Morris' Article on Richard Barnfield ...," Publications of the Modern Language Association, 76 (1961), 150-3.

On names by R. Barnfield and others.

---, See: 804.

1140 Stäuble, Eduard
Name ist nicht Schall und Rauch. Die Poesie der Spitz- und Übernamen. Eine Radio Hörfolge. St. Gallen, 1958.

On German nicknames.

1141 Stavenhagen, Lee
"The Name Tadzio in 'Der Tod in Venedig'," German Quarterly, 35 (1962), 20-3.

On the name "Tadzio" by Thomas Mann.

1142 Steadman, J. M.
    "Simkin's Camus Nose: A Latin Pun in the
    Reeve's Tale?" Modern Language Notes, 75
    (1960), 4-8.

    On names by Chaucer.

1143 Steele, R. B.
    "Names in the Metrical Technique of the Aeneid,"
    The New York Latin Leaflet, 6, No. 145 (March
    26, 1906), 1-2; No. 146 (April 2, 1906), 1-3.

    On names by Vergil.

1144 Štefanic, V.
    "Dobrinjski pjesnik-glagoljaš Ivan Uravic,
    1662-1732," Krčki zbornik, 1 (1970), 201-22.

    On names in the work of Ivan Uravic.

1145 Steger, Hugo
    Probleme der Namenforschung im deutschsprachigen
    Raum. Darmstadt, Wissenschaftliche Buchgesell-
    schaft, 1977.

    A collection of essays on onomastics.

1146 Stein, Gertrude
    Four in America. New Haven, Yale Univesity
    Press, 1947.

    On names, passim.

1147 Steinberg, Clarence
    "The Clever Name Game on the Way to Canterbury
    and Beyond: Onomastica dramatica Chauceriana."

    A paper read at the Kalamazoo Conference, 1972.
    See also Robert A. Pratt's reassessed version
    in Speculum, 47 (1972), 422-2, and 646-68.

1148 Steiner, Ernst
    "Von der Namengebung des Dichtes. Ein Gang
    durch Jeremias Gotthelfs Werke," Sprachspiegel,
    12 (1956), 68-76.

    On names by J. Gotthelf.

1149 Steinle, Gisela B.
Namen, Autonomasien und qualifizierende
Personenbezeichnungen im epischen Werk
Hartmann's von Aue. McGill University,
1975.

A dissertation on the names in the works of
Hartmann von Aue.

1150 Stemmler, T.
"Zur Deutung der Eigennamen in den Komödien
Christopher Frys," Archiv für das Studium
neueren Sprachen und Literaturen, 115 (1963),
198-201.

On names in the comedies of Fry.

Stepanova, A. G.
See: 1344.

1151 Stephens, Edna B.
"Literary Names in English Literature," in Of
Edsels and Marauders. Ed. by F. Tarpley and A.
Moseley. Commerce, Texas, Names Institute Press,
1971. (South Central Names Institute Publication
No. 1).

See p. 95.

1152 Stephens, Thomas Arthur
Proverb Literature: A Bibliography of Works
Relating to Proverbs. Ed. by Wilfrid Bonser.
London, Glaisber, 1930.

1153 Steub, Ludwig
Die oberdeutschen Familiennamen. München,
Oldenbourg, 1870.

On German family names.

1154 Stevenson, Lionel
"Names in Pickwick," The Dickensian, 32
(1936), 241-4.

On names by Dickens.

1155 Stewart, George R.
"And Adam Gave Names - A Consideration of Name-
lore in Antiquity," Names, 6 (1958), 1-10.

On Hebrew and Greek names.

1156 ---, "An Interview on Names," Names, 9 (1961),
53-7.

On the naming of his characters; interviewed
by J. M. Backus.

Stiehl, Ruth
See: 758.

Stier, Hans Erich
See: 758.

1157 Stöcklein, Paul
"Nachwort," Goethes Werke. Gedenkausgabe, 14
vols. Hamburg, Wegner, 1946-60.

See Vol. 9, pp. 714-6, on names in the "Wahl-
verwandtschaften," by Goethe.

1158 ---, Wege zum späten Goethe. Darmstadt, Wissenschaftliche Buchgesellschaft, 1970.

On names by Goethe, see pp. 68-80.

1159 Stokes, Francis Griffin
A Dictionary of the Characters and Proper Names
in the Works of Shakespeare. With notes on the
sources and dates of the plays and poems. London, Harrap, 1949.

First published in 1924.

1160 Stoltenberg, Hans Lorenz
Etruskische Gottnamen. Leverkusen, Gottschalk,
1957. (Sammlung praktischer Lehr- und Hand-
bücher auf wissenschaftlicher Grundlage. 2.
Reihe: Philologie 1. Gruppe: Allgemeine
Sprachwissenschaft, 4. Etruskischer Wortschatz
Bd. 1)

On Etruscan names of gods.

1161 Stone, Edward
"James's 'Jungle': The Seasons," University of Kansas City Review, 21 (1954), 142-4.

1162 Stone, Harry
"Dickens and the Naming of Sam Weller," The Dickensian, 56 (Winter 1960), 47-9.

1163 Stopes, Charlotte Carmichael
"The Earliest Official Record of Shakespeare's Name," Jahrbuch der Deutschen Shakespeare-Gesellschaft, 32 (1896), 182-9.

1164 ---, Shakespeare's Family. London, Stock, 1901.

On Shakespeare's name, see Pt. 1, pp. 1-3.

1165 Storbeck, Ludwig
Die Nennung des eigenen Namens bei den deutschen Geschichtschreibern des Mittelalters. Halle, Kaemmerer, 1910.

A dissertation. On self-naming among German historical writers of the Middle Ages.

1166 Störing, H.
Untersuchungen zu den Personennamen in der altfranzösischen Literatur. Münster, 1974.

A dissertation. On personal names in Old French literature.

1167 Storms, G.
Compounded Names of Peoples in Beowulf. A Study in the Diction of a Great Poet. Utrecht, Nijmegen, 1957.

---, See: 744.

1168 Stotsenburg, John Hawley
An Impartial Study of the Shakespeare Title. Louisville, Morton, 1904.

On Shakespeare's name, see pp. 192-203.

1169 Stratford, Philip
        "Unlocking the Potting Shed," The Kenyon
        Review, 24 (Winter 1962), 129-43.

        On Graham Greene's names.

1170 Straubinger, O. Pual
        "Der wahre Jakob," Names, 1 (1953), 112-4.

        On German proverbs.

1171 ---, Given Names in German Proverbs. University
        of California, Los Angeles, 1946.

        A dissertation.

1172 ---, "Name Clues in Proverbs (Allusion to a Persona
        Name)," Names, 9 (1961), 112-6.

1173 ---, "Names in Popular Saying," Names, 3 (1955),
        157-64.

1174 Strolle, Jon
        "The Names of God in Saint Teresa," Literary
        Onomastics Studies, 4 (1977), 115-30.

1175 Studien zur Namenkunde und Sprachgeographie. Fest-
        schrift für Karl Finsterwalder zum 70. Geburts-
        tag. Hrsg. von Wolfgang Meid, Hermann M.
        Ölberg, Hans Schmeja. Innsbruck, Institut
        für vergleichende Sprachwissenschaft der Uni-
        versität, 1971. (Innsbrucker Beiträge zur
        Kulturwissenschaft, Bd. 16)

        A collection of essays on onomastics and
        language geography.

1176 Stümpel, Gustav
        Name und Nationalität der Germanen. Neue
        Untersuchungen zu Poseidonios, Cäsar und
        Tacitus. Leipzig, 1932. Reprint: Aalen,
        Scientia, 1963. (Klio Reihe 25/12)

        On the name and nationality of the Germans.
        Also on Posidonius, Caesar, and Tacitus.

Sturn, Johann
        See: 393.

1177 Sturtevant, A. M.
        "Etymological Comments on Certain Words and
        Names in the Elder Edda," Publications of the
        Modern Language Association, 66 (1951), 278-91.

1178 ---, "Etymologies of Old Norse Proper Names Used
        as Poetric Designations," Modern Language
        Notes, 64 (1949), 486-90.

1179 Sugden, Edward Holdsworth
        A Topographical Dictionary to the Works of
        Shakespeare and His Fellow Dramatists. London,
        Longmans, 1925. (Publications of the University
        of Manchester, No. 168).

        See also reprint: 1969.

1180 Summers, William
        How to Coin Winning Names. New York, Arco,
        1951.

1181 Swanson, Donald Carl Eugene
        A Characterization of the Roman Poetic Ono-
        masticon. University Park, Pennsylvania State
        University Press, 1970.

        On Latin names.

1182 ---, The Names in Roman Verse. A lexicon and reverse
        index of all proper names of history, mythology,
        and geography found in the classical Roman
        poets. Madison, University of Wisconsin Press,
        1967.

        On Latin names.

     ---, See: 159, 766, 1025.

1183 Syme, R.
        "Personal Names in (Tacitus) Annals I-VI,"
        Journal of Roman Studies, 39 (1949), 6-18.

1184 Szilágyi, Ferenc
"A magyar szó költészete: Mucsa, Piripócs, Kukutyin - Földrajzi nevek stilisztikája," Magyar Hirek, 29 (March 27, 1976), 12.

On Hungarian literary toponyma.

1185 Szoboszlay, A.
"A tulajdonnevek Németh László drámáiban," Magyar Nyelvjárások, 17 (1971), 159-80.

On names in the dramas of L. Neméth, the Hungarian writer.

1186 Szymanowska, Irena
"Personennamen in zwei Werken von Majakovskij, Zpravodaj Mistopisné Komise Československé Akademie Věd, 16 (1975), 202-7.

On names by Majakovskij.

1187 Taič, R. U.
"Opyt antroponimičeskogo slovarja pisatelja,"
Antroponimika (1970), 314-9.

A dictionary of personal names.

1188 ---, "Specifika proizvedenija i onomastičeskij
slovar pisatelja," Respublikanska Onomastyčna
Konferencija Kyjiv, 4 (1969), 157-9.

A dictionary of onomastics.

1189 Takeoka, T.
"Mikawa Futamimichi kô," Chuôdai Kokubun/Revue
de littérature de l'Université Chuô, Tokyo, 15
(1971),

On toponyma in Old Japanese poems from the Aichi
district, see pp. 12-21.

1190 Takeshita, K.
Bungaku iseki jiten - sanbunhen. Tokyo, Edit.
Tokyodo, 1971.

A dictionary of names in prose. See also Vol.
1 of poetry, 1968.

1191 Tamke, A. R.
"'Gat' in Gatsby: Neglected Aspect of a Novel,"
Modern Fiction Studies, 14 (1968-9), 443-5.

On the above name in the work of F. Scott
Fitzgerald.

---, See: 642.

1192 Tanner, William E.
"Charactonyms in the 'Alexandria Quartet':
Threads in a Tapestry," in Of Edsels and
Marauders. Ed. by F. Tarpley and A. Moseley.
Commerce, Texas, Names Institute Press, 1971.
(South Central Names Institute Publication
No. 1)

On names by Lawrence Durrell, see pp. 123-6.

1193 Tantsch, Werner
       "Meister Hämmerlein," Beiträge zur Namen-
       forschung, 7 (1956), 281-93.

       On names of devils, hangmen, charlatans,
       etc., in literature from the sixteenth to
       the nineteenth centuries.

     Tarnavets'ka, Iraida Gerus
        See: Gerus-Tarnavets'ka, Iraida

1194 Tarnellr, J.
       "Die Hofnamen in den alten Kirchspielen
       Deutschhofen - Eggental und Vels am Schlern,"
       Archiv für Österreichische Geschichte, 106
       (1915), 1-117.

       On names of courts in old church plays.

1195 Tarpley, Fred, ed.
       Love and Wrestling, Butch and O. K. Presented
       by the Department of Literature and Languages,
       East Texas State University in cooperation with
       the American Name Society. Commerce, Texas,
       Names Institute Press, 1973. (South Central
       Names Institute Publication No. 2)

1196 ---, Naughty Names. Presented by the Department of
       Literature and Languages, East Texas State
       University in cooperation with the American
       Name Society. Commerce, Texas, Names Institute
       Press, 1975. (South Central Names Institute
       Publication No. 4)

1197 ---, They Had to Call It Something. Presented by
       the Department of Literature and Languages, East
       Texas State University in cooperation with the
       American Name Society. Commerce, Texas, Names
       Institute Press, 1974. (South Central Names
       Institute Publication No. 3)

1198 ---, and Ann Moseley
       Of Edsels and Marauders. Presented by the
       Department of English, East Texas State Uni-
       versity in cooperation with the American Name
       Society, Commerce, Texas, Names Institute Press
       1971. (South Central Names Institute Publica-
       tion No. 1)

---, See: 69, 74, 134, 144, 220, 221, 232, 382, 412, 515, 711, 917, 1072, 1078, 1099, 1114, 1115, 1157, 1192, 1203, 1207, 1208, 1225, 1242, 1251, 1252, 1253, 1254.

Taszycki, V.
See: 380.

1199 Tau, Max
Der assoziative Faktor in der Landschafts- und Ortsdarstellung Theodor Fontanes. Oldenburg, Schulz, 1928. (Forschungen zur Literatur-, Theater- und Zeitungswissenschaft, Bd. 1)

On names by Fontane, see pp. 65-7.

1200 Taylor, Archer
"Grete's Bad Name," Modern Language Notes, 58 (1943), 452-4.

On connotations of the name Grete, including in Goethe's "Faust."

1201 ---, "Investigations of English Proverbs, Proverbial and Conventional Phrases, Oaths and Cliches," Journal of American Folklore, 65 (1952), 255-66.

1202 ---, "The Use of Proper Names in Wellerism and Folk Tales," Western Folklore, 18 (1959), 287-93.

1203 Taylor, Balma C.
"Towns, Poets, and Mythology," in Of Edsels and Marauders. Ed. by F. Tarpley and A. Moseley. Commerce, Texas, Names Institute Press, 1971. (South Central Names Institute Publication No. 1)

See pp. 58-65 on mythology reflected in place-names of America.

1204 Taylor, P. B.
"Gawain's Garland of Girdle and Name," English Studies, 55 (1974), 6-14.

1205 Telle, Joachim
  "'Tristans Wasser' und 'Morolfs Wein'. Zur
  Verwendung von Personennamen in mittelalterlichen Fachtermini zusammengesetzter Arznei-
  mittel," Beiträge zur Namenforschung, 6 (1971)
  69-78.

  On the use of drug terminology and its influence on personal names in German heroic poetry.

1206 Tennyson, G. B.
  Sartor Called Resartur. The Genesis, Structure
  and Style of Thomas Carlyle's First Major Work
  Princeton University Press, 1965.

  On names, see pp. 146, 220-2.

1207 Terrell, Dahlia
  "Humor and Hysteria: Names in Flannery O'Con-
  nor's Fiction," in They Had to Call it Something
  Ed. by F. Tarpley. Commerce, Texas, Names
  Institute Press, 1974. (South Central Names
  Institute Publication No. 3)

  See pp. 125-9.

1208 ---, "Names and the Nihilistic Mood in 'The Sound
  and the Fury', in Labeled for Life.' Ed. by
  F. Tarpley. Commerce, Texas, Names Institute
  Press, 1977. (South Central Names Institute
  Publication No. 5)

  See pp. 69-72 on names by Faulkner.

1209 Théry, J.
  "L'emploi des noms patronymiques dans les
  oeuvres littéraires," Mercure de France,
  292 (1939), 606-11.

  On patronymic names in literature.

1210 Thieberger, Richard
  "Hooofmannsthal?" Etudes Germaniques, 27
  (1972), 608-9.

  On Hofmannsthal's name.

1211 Thilo, Ulrich
Die Ortsnamen in der altarabischen Poesie.
Ein Beitrag zur vor- und frühislamischen
Dichtung und zur historischen Topographie
Nordarabiens. Wiesbaden, Harrassowitz, 1958.
(Schriften der Max Freiherr von Oppenheim-
Stiftung, Heft 3)

On toponyma in Old Arabic poetry.

1212 Thomas, P.
"Noms typiques, employés par métonymie dans
la littérature latine," Académie Royale de
Belgique. Classe des Lettres et des Sciences
Morales et Politiques, Bulletin, Ser. 13, No.
2 (1927), 46-64.

On names in Latin literature.

1213 Thomas Ralph
Handbook of Fictitious Names. Being a guide
to authors, chiefly in the lighter literature
of the 19th century, who have written under
assumed names; and to literary forgers, im-
posters, plagiarist, and imitators, by Olphar
Hamst (pseud.) London, Smith, 1868. Reprint:
Leipzig, Zentralantiquariat, 1977.

Thorpe, Clarence De Witt
See: 524.

1214 Tibon, Gutierre
Diccionario etimologico comparado de nombres
proprios de persona. Mexico, Union Tipografica,
1956.

A dictionary of proper names.

1215 ---, "The Name Dante," Names, 1 (1953), 208.

1216 Tiefenbach, Heinrich
"Der Name der Wormser in Summarium Heinrici.
Bemerkungen zur Neuedition des Glossars mit
Beiträgen zur Lokalisierung, Datierung und
Werktitel," Beiträge zur Namenforschung, 10
(1975), 241-80.

On the name "Wormser" in the "Summarian Heinrici."

1217 Tobler-Meyer, W.
Deutsche Familiennamen nach ihren Entstehung
und Bedeutung. Zürich, Müller, 1894.

On the origin and meaning of German family
names.

1218 Tolman, Albert Harris
The Views About Hamlet and Other Essays. Bos-
ton, Houghton, 1904. Reprint: New York, AMS
Press, 1973.

On the usage of names by Shakespeare; also
includes references to English personal names
in general.

1219 Torbert, Eugene Charles
A Study of Place-Names in the Works of Cer-
vantes. University of North Carolina at Chapel
Hill, 1974.

A dissertation.

Tornow, Walter Robert
See: Robert-Tornow, Walter

1220 Törnqvist, E.
"Personal Nomenclature in the Plays of O'Neill,
Modern Drama, 8 (1966), 362-73.

1221 Törö, Gy.
"Petrovits-töl Petöfi-ig," Irodalomtörténeti
közlemények, 67 (1963), 598-9.

On the variation of Petöfi, the Hungarian poet
name.

1222 Torrance, Catherine
The Names of the Warriors in Vergil's Aeneid
VII-XII; His Sources and His Methods. Univer-
sity of Chicago, 1926.

A dissertation.

1223 Tournier, Paul
      The Naming of Persons. New York, Harper, 1975.

1224 Toynbee, Paget Jackson
      A Dictionary of Proper Names and Notable Matters
      in the Works of Dante. New ed. rev. by Charles
      S. Singleton. Oxford, Clarendon, 1968.

      Originally published in 1898. See also the
      Oxford 1914 edition under the title: Concise
      Dictionary of Proper Names and Notable Matters
      in the Works of Dante.

   Trask, Willard R.
      See: 229.

   Trenchmann, E. J.
      See: 789.

   Tschirch, Fritz
      See: 616.

1225 Tuerk, Richard
      "Tommy Wilhelm - Wilhelm Adler: Names in
      'Seize the Day'," in Naughty Names. Ed. by
      F. Tarpley, Commerce, Texas. Names Institute
      Press, 1975. (South Central Names Institute
      Publication No. 4)

      On names by Saul Bellow see pp. 27-34.

1226 Turville-Petre, J. E.
      "Hengest and Horsa," Saga Book, 14 (1956-7),
      273-90.

      An interpretation of the above names.

   Tyler, Richard W.
      See: 46, 53, 797, 802, 955.

1227 Tyroff, Siegmar
    Namen bei Thomas Mann in den 'Erzählungen'
    und den Romanen 'Buddenbrooks', 'Königliche
    Hoheit', 'Der Zauberberg'. Bern, Lang, 1975.
    (Europäische Hochschulschriften, Reihe 1,
    Deutsche Literatur und Germanistik, Bd.
    102)

    On names by Thomas Mann.

---, See: 111.

1228 Ulewicz, Tadeusz
"W sprawie humanistycznych pseudonimóv
literackich," Onomastica (Wroclaw), 4
(1958), 139-47.

On literary pseudonyms.

1229 Ullman, B. L.
"Proper Names in Plautus, Terence, and
Menander," Classical Philology, 11 (1916),
61-4.

1230 Unbegaun, Boris Ottokar
Russian Surnames. Oxford, Clarendon Press,
1972.

On "Literary Surnames," see pp. 244-55.

---, See: 966.

Untermann, Jürgen
See: 1054.

1231 Urbach, O.
"Eigennamen als Begriffe," Muttersprache, 53
(1938), 250-(?).

On proper names as concepts.

Urban, E.
See: 697.

1232 Utešený, S.
"Setkáni spisovatele J. Škvoreckého s živou
Amerikou - ve jmenech (Podle 'Dospisu z USA
I-XXX, Svet práce, 1969)," Zpravodaj Misto-
pisné Komise Československé Akademie Věd, 11
(1970), 410-21.

On an encounter with American names.

1233 Utley, Francis Lee
"From the Dinnsenchas to Proust: The Folklore of Placenames in Literature," <u>Names</u>, 16
(1968), 273-93.

1234 ---, "The Linguistic Component of Onomastics,"
<u>Names</u>, 11 (1963), 145-76.

1235 ---, "The Names of the Knights of the Round Table,"
<u>Names</u>, 23 (1975), 194-214.

On Arthurian names.

---, See: 820.

1236 Väänänen, V.
"Grobis, Gros Bis et Raminagrobis," Revue
de Linguistique Roumaine, 34 (1970), 167-78.

On interpretation of the above names.

1237 Vaganay, H.
"Quartre noms propres dans la litterature:
Délie, Philothée, Ophélie, Pasithée,"
Revue de Littérature Comparée, 15 (1935),
279-88.

On the above names in literature.

1238 Vajay, S. de
"Rayonnement de la 'Chanson de Roland'. Le
couple anthroponymique 'Roland et Olivier' en
Hongrie médiévale," Moyen Age, 68 (1962),
321-9.

On names in the "Chanson de Roland" and
"Roland et Olivier."

1239 Vance, N.
"Charlotte Brontë's Mr. Brocklehurst," Notes
and Queries, 24 (1977), 25.

van der Kolk, H.
See: Kolk, H. van der

1240 Van Doren, Carl
"Good Names," in his The Roving Critic, New
York, Knopf, 1923.

See pp. 133-41 on his analysis of names.

van Eerde, J.
See: Eerde, J. van

van Egmond, Peter
See: Egmond, Peter van

van Els, T. J. M.
See: Els, T. J. M. van

1241 van Emden, W. G.
"Rolandiana et Oliveriana, faits et hypoth-
èses," Romania, 92 (1971), 507-31.

On analysis of names in Roland and Olivier.

van Langendonck, Willy
See: Langendonck, Willy van

1242 Vann, Don J.
"Dickens and Charley Bates," in Of Edsels and
Marauders. Ed. by F. Tarpley and A. Moseley.
Commerce, Texas, Names Institute Press, 1971.
(South Central Names Institute Publication No.
1)

See pp. 117-22.

van Windekens, Albert J.
See: Windekens, Albert J. van

van Winkle, Edgar S.
See: Winkle, Edgar S. van

1243 Vasmer, M.
"Studien zur russischen Volksepik," Zeitschrift
für slawische Philologie, 29 (1961), 382-8.

On names in Russian epic literature.

---, See: 966.

Verne Crum, Earl Le
See: Crum, Earl Le Verne

1244 Veselovskii, Stepan Borisovich
Onomastikon. Moskva, Nauka, 1974.

A dictionary of Russian personal names.

Vizetelly, Ernst A.
See: 1346.

von Bonsdorff, Ingrid
    See: Bonsdorff, Ingrid von

von Krockow, Peter
    See: Krockow, Peter von

von Oppen, Elisabeth Lotte
    See: Oppen, Elisabeth Lotte von

von Orelli, Johan Kaspar
    See: Orelli, Johann Kaspar von

von Polenz, Peter
    See: Polenz, Peter von

von Propper, Maximilian
    See: Propper, Maximilian von

von Wilpert, Gero
    See: Wilpert, Gero von

1245 Vouk, V.
    "Shakespearean Names in Serbo-Croation
    Translations," _Studia Romanica et Anglica
    Zagrebiensia_ (December 1960), 191-8.

1246 Vries, J. de
    "Le nom de Stendhal," _Vie et Language_, 97
    (1960), 209.

    On Stendhal's name.

1247 Vroonen, Eugène
    _Les noms des personnes dans le monde. Anthro-
    ponomie universelle comparée._ Bruxelles, Ed.
    de la Librarie Encyclopédique, 1967.

    A comparative study of personal names.

1248 Vuletič, B.
"Smisao ličnih imena i naziva u Krležinoj
'Kraljevskoj ugarskoj domobranskoj noveli',"
<u>Umjetnost riječi</u>, 14/2 (1970), 259-65.

On personal names in the works of Krleža.

1249 Wade, G. E.
       "Character Names in Some of Tirso's Comedies,"
       Hispanic Review, 36 (1968), 1-34.

       On names by Téllez.

1250 Wade, Ira Own
       "Voltaire's Name," Publications of the Modern
       Language Association, 44 (1929), 546-64.

1251 Wages, Jack D.
       "Benjamin Franklin: Onomatologist," in
       Naughty Names. Ed. by F. Tarpley. Commerce,
       Texas, Names Institute Press, 1975. (South
       Central Names Institute Publication No. 4)

       See pp. 21-6.

1252 ---, "From Urth to Venas: Names in Recent American
       Science-Fiction," in Labeled for Life. Ed. by
       F. Tarpley. Commerce, Texas, Names Institute
       Press, 1977. (South Central Names Institute
       Publication No. 5)

       See pp. 63-7.

1253 ---, "Names in Eudora Welty's Fiction: An Onomato-
       logical Prolegomenon," in Love and Wrestling,
       Butch and O. K. Ed. by F. Tarpley. Commerce,
       Texas, Names Institute Press, 1973. (South
       Central Names Institute Publication No. 2)

       See pp. 65-72.

1254 ---, "Names in the Fiction of Thomas Pynchon," in
       They Had to Call it Something. Ed. by F. Tar-
       pley. Commerce, Texas, Names Institute Press,
       1974. (South Central Names Institute Publica-
       tion No. 3)

       See pp. 131-5.

1255 Wagner, Herbert
       "A Review of S. Gutenbrunner's 'Von Hilde-
       brand ...'," Beiträge zur Namenforschung,
       12 (1977), 295-8.

---, See: 428.

1256 Wagner, Leopold
     More About Names. London, Unwin, 1893. Re-
     print: Detroit, Gale, 1968.

     On names, general.

1257 ---, Names and Their Meaning. A Book for the
     Curious. London, Unwin, 1893. Reprint:
     Detroit, Gale, 1968.

     See also the 1977 edition.

1258 Waldfreund, J. E.
     "Sprichwörtlich angewendete Vornamen und
     damit verbundene Kinderreime," Die deutschen
     Mundarten, 3 (1856), 314-7.

     On first names in children's rhymes.

1259 Walker, Ralph S.
     "A Review of V. A. Nikonov's 'Imja i obshestvo',"
     Names, 23 (1975), 303.

     On names in literature.

     ---, See: 850.

1260 Walkley, Arthur Bingham
     More Prejudice. London, Heinemann, 1923.

     On literary onomastics, see pp. 196-200.

1261 Waller, E.
     "Ještě ke jménům Tunna a Gommon v českých
     legendách a kronikach," Scando-Slavica, 7
     (1961), 133-57.

     On the above names in Czech legends and chron-
     icles.

1262 Walsh, William Shepard
        Handy-Book of Literary Curiosities.   Phila-
        delphia, Lippincott, 1892.

        On names in fiction, see pp. 785-9.

1263 ---, Heroes and Heroines of Fiction, Modern Prose
        and Poetry. Famous characters and famous names
        in novels, romances, poems, and dramas, clas-
        sified, analyzed and criticised with supple-
        mentary citations from the best authorities.
        Philadelphia, Lippincott, 1914.

        See also the 1931 edition in 2 volumes.

    Walther, Hans
        See: 274, 822.

1264 Wapnewski, Peter
        Hartmann von Aue.   3., ergänzte Auflage.
        Stuttgart, Metzler, 1972. (Sammlung Metzler,
        17)

        On interpretations of names, see pp. 3-10.

1265 Wardropper, B. W.
        "A Review of 'Los nombres ...' by Morley-
        Tyler,' Modern Language Notes, 76 (1961),
        934-8.

1266 ---, "A Review of 'Los nombres ...' by Morley-
        Tyler," Romanic Philology, 17 (1963), 511-6.

        On names by Lope de Vega.

    ---, See: 802.

1267 Ware, N. J.
        "Testimony of Classical Names in Support of
        Metrical Regularity in the Libro de Alexandre,"
        Hispanic Review, 35 (1967), 211-26.

    Warner, Sylvia Towsend
        See: 933.

1268 Wasiolek, Edward
      "Yanko Goorall. A Note on Name Symbolism in
      Conrad's 'Amy Foster'," <u>Modern Language Notes</u>,
      71 (1956), 418-9.

1269 Wasserzieher, Ernst
      <u>Hans und Grete</u>. 2500 Vornamen erklärt. 17.,
      neubearbeitete Auflage von Paul Melchers, Bonn,
      Dümmler, 1967.

      On German names. Earlier edition also by Paul
      Harthum.

1270 Watanabe, M.
      "Le nom d'Ysé. Le mythe solaire japonais et
      la genèse du personnage," <u>Revue de l'Histoire
      Littéraire de la France</u>, 69 (1969), 74-92.

      On names by P. Claudel.

1271 Watt, Ian P.
      "The Naming of Characters in Defoe, Richardson,
      and Fielding," <u>The Review of English Studies</u>,
      25 (1949), 322-38.

1272 ---, <u>The Rise of the Novel. Studies in Defoe, Rich-
      ardson, and Fielding</u>. Berkeley, University of
      California Press, 1964.

      On names, see pp. 236-7.

      ---, See: 185, 261.

1273 Watts, George Byron
      "Voltaire's Change of Name," <u>Modern Language
      Notes</u>, 37 (1923), 329-33.

1274 Weber, Gottfried, and Werner Hoffmann
      <u>Niebelungenlied</u>. 4. ergänzte Auflage. Stutt-
      gart, Metzler, 1974. (Sammlung Metzler, 7)

      On names see pp. 28-46, 68-70, and 91-3.

1275 Weekley, Ernest
Jack and Jill. A Study in Our Christian Names.
Ann Arbor, Gryphon, 1971.

1276 ---, The Romance of Names. New York, Blom, 1971.

1277 ---, Surnames. London, Murray, 1916.

See also later edition.

1278 ---, Words and Names. Freeport, Books for Libraries,
1971.

1279 Weever, Jacqueline Elinor de
A Dictionary of Classical, Mythological and
Sideral Names in the Works of Geoffrey Chaucer.
University of Pennsylvania, 1971.

A dissertation.

Wegener, G.
See: 707.

1280 Wehling, M. M.
"Marlowe's Mnemonic Nominology with Especial
Reference to Tamburlaine," Modern Language
Notes, 73 (1958), 243-7.

Wehrli, Max
See: 1056.

1281 Weidhorn, Manfred
"The Rose and Its Name: On Denomination in
Othello, Romeo and Juliet, Julius Caesar,"
Texas Studies in Literature and Language,
11 (1969), 671-86.

On names by Shakespeare.

1282 Weinberg, Kurt
Kafkas Dichtungen. Die Travestien des Mythos.
Bern, Francke, 1963.

On individual names, see the index.

1283 Weingarten, Samuel
      "The Name of King in Richard II," <u>College
      English</u>, 27 (1966), 536-41.

      On names by Shakespeare.

1284 Weinhold, Karl
      <u>Die Personennamen des Kieler Stadtbuches von
      1264-88</u>. Kiel, Mohr, 1860.

      On personal names in the city book of Kiel.

1285 Weinreich, Otto
      <u>Der Trug des Nektanebos. Wandlungen eines
      Novellenstoffes</u>. Leipzig, Teubner, 1911.

      On literary onomastics, passim.

1286 Weintraub, S.
      "'Humors' Names in Shaw's Prentice Novels,"
      <u>Names</u>, 5 (1957), 222-5.

1287 Weller, Karl
      "Die Nibelungenstrasse," <u>Zeitschrift für
      deutsches Altertum und deutsche Literatur</u>,
      70 (1933), 49-66.

      On toponyma in the Nibelungen.

1288 Wells, Evelyn
      <u>A Treasury of Names</u>. New York, Duell, 1946.

      On personal names, general.

1289 Wentscher, Erich
      <u>Die Rufnamen des deutschen Volkes</u>. Eine
      Studie mit einem Verzeichnis unserer gebrauch-
      lichen Rufnamen nebst deren Wortsinn. Halle,
      Waisenhaus, 1928.

      On German names.

1290 Werner, Waltraud
Die männlichen Personennamen in den bulgarischen Volksliedern. Ein Beitrag zur bulgarischen Anthroponomie. Wiesbaden. Harrassowitz,
1965. (Berlin, Freie Universität. Osteuropa
Institut. Slavistische Veröffentlichungen,
Bd. 33)

On masculine personal names in Bulgarian folksongs.

1291 Wernicke, Ewald
"Vor- und Zunamen aus mittelalterlichen Deutungen in schlesischen Urkunden," Anzeiger für
Kunde der deutschen Vorzeit, 28 (1881), 78-80.

On German names from the Middle Ages.

1292 West, G. D.
An Index of Proper Names in French Arthurian
Verse Romances 1150-1300. Toronto, University
of Toronto Press, 1969.

---, See: 325, 1001, 1105.

1293 West, Robert H.
"The Names of Milton's Angels," Studies in
Philology, 47 (1950), 210-23.

1294 Westburg, B.
"His Allegorical Way of Expressing It: Civil
War and Psychic Conflict in Oliver Twist and
A Child's History," Studies in the Novel, 6
(1974), 27-37.

On names by Dickens.

1295 Weydt, G.
"Zur Deutung und Namengebung des 'Helmbrecht',"
Zeitschrift für deutsche Philologie, 62 (1937),
264-7.

On the name "Helmbrecht."

1296 Whatley, E. G.
"Old English Onomastics and Narrative Art:
Elene 1062," _Modern Philology_, 73 (1975),
109-20.

Wheeler, Charles G.
See: 1299.

1297 Wheeler, William Adolphus
A Dictionary of the Noted Names of Fiction.
Including also familiar pseudonyms, surnames,
bestowed on eminent men, and analogous popular
appellations often referred to in literature
and conversation. London, Bell, 1892.

1298 ---, _An Explanatory and Pronouncing Dictionary of_
the Noted Names of Fiction. Boston, Ticknor,
1865.

See also later edition.

1299 ---, _Familiar Allusions._ A hand-book of miscellaneous information, including the names of
celebrated statues, paintings, palaces, country
seats, ruins, churches, ships, streets, clubs,
natural curiosities, and the like. Ed. by
Charles G. Wheeler. Boston, Osgood, 1882.

1300 White, Richard Grant
Shakespeare's Scholar. Being historical and
critical studies of his text, characters, and
commentators, with an examination of Mr.
Collier's folio of 1632. New York, Appleton,
1854.

On Shakespeare's name, see pp. 678-80.

1301 Whitehead, Lee M.
"Alma Renamed Lena in Conrad's Victory,"
English Language Notes, 3 (1965), 55-7.

1302 Whitelock, Dorothy
"Scandinavian Personal Names in the Liber Vitae
of Thorney Abbey," _Viking Society for Northern_
Reseach. London. _Saga Book of the Viking Club_,
12 (1940), 127-53.

1303 Wiacek, Wilhelmina M.
Lexique des noms géographiques et ethniques
dans les poésies des troubadours des XII et
XIII siècles. Paris, Nizet, 1968.

On Provençal names.

1304 Wilkins, Ernest H.
"The Naming of Rodomont," Modern Language
Notes, 70 (1955) 596-9.

On names by Boiardo.

1305 Wilkon, A.
Nazewnictwo w utworach Stefana Żeromskiego.
Prace Onomastyczne Pan 16, Wroczlaw, 1970.

On onomastics in the works of S. Żeromski.

1306 Will, Frederic
"From Naming to Fiction-Making," in Literature
Inside Out. Ten Speculative Essays. Cleveland,
Western Reserve University Press, 1966.

See pp. 3-15.

1307 Willberg, W.
"Abgewertete Vornamen," Muttersprache, 75
(1965), 330-42.

On German first names.

1308 Williams, Harry F.
"A Review of 'Table des noms ...' by F.
Flutre," Romanic Philology, 17 (1963), 485-6.

On French names in the chansons de geste.

---, See: 326, 853.

1309 Willoughby, Leonard Ashley
"'Name ist Schall und Rauch'. On the Signifi-
cance of Names for Goethe," German Life and
Letters, 16 (1962-3), 294-307.

1310 --- "Namen und Namengeben bei Goethe," in Goethe
und die Tradition. Hrsg. von Hans Reiss.
Frankfurt, Athenäum, 1972. (Wissenschaftliche
Paperbacks, Literaturwissenschaft, 19)

On names by Goethe, see pp. 259-81.

1311 ---, What's in a Name? London, Modern Language
Association, 1962. (A. E. Twentyman Lecture,
1)

On personal names; general.

1312 Willson, R. F.
"Falstaff in 1 Henry IV: What's in a Name?
Shakespeare Journal, 27 (1976), 199-200.

On the above name by Shakespeare.

1313 Wilpert, Gero von
Sachwörterbuch der Literatur. 5., verb.
und erw. Aufl. Stuttgart, Kröner, 1969.

A dictionary of literary terms. On descrip-
tive names, see p. 509. See also other editions.

1314 Wilson, E.
"Gromylyoun (Gromwell) in Pearl," Notes and
Queries, 18 (1971), 42-4.

1315 Wilson, Robert H.
"Malory's Naming of Minor Characters," The
Journal of English and German Philology, 42
(1943), 364-85.

Wilson, R. M.
See: 952.

1316 Wimmer, Rainer
Der Eigenname im Deutschen. Ein Beitrag zu
seiner linguistischen Beschreibung. Tübingen,
Niemeyer, 1973. (Linguistische Arbeiten, 11)

On linguistic aspects of German proper names.

1317 Windekens, Albert J. van
"The 'Selloi' at Dodona," Names, 9 (1961)
91-4.

On the above name by Homer.

1318 Winkle, Edgar S. van
"The Spelling of Shakespeare's Name," The
International Review, 5 (1878), 690-4.

1319 Winkler, Johan
De Nederlandsche geslachtsnamen in oorsprong,
geschiedenis en beteekenis. Haarlem, Willink,
1885.

On personal names of the Netherlands.

1320 Wintson, M.
"Bussy d'Ambois as Sir Ambo," Notes and Queries,
23 (1976), 214-5.

On the above name by George Chapman.

1321 Winter, Elke
"Der Siedlungsname Hatzenport und die westeuro-
päischen port-Namen," Beiträge zur Namenforschung, (Beihefte 1), 1969.

On names in the Pidriks Saga, see p. 32.

1322 Wise, Goerge
The Autograph of William Shakespeare. With
facsimiles of his signature as appended to
various legal documents; together with 4000
ways of spelling the name according to English
orthography. Philadelphia, Abel, 1869.

1323 Wisniewski, Roswitha
Die Darstellung des Niflungenunterganges in
der Thidrekssaga. Eine quellenkritische Untersuchung. Tübingen, Niemeyer, 1961. (Hermaea,
Germanistische Forschungen, Bd. 9)

On names see pp. 253-6. See also dissertation;
Freie Universität, Berlin.

1324 ---, <u>Kudrun</u>. 2., überarbeitete Auflage. Stuttgart,
     <u>Metzler</u>, 1969. (Sammlung Metzler, 32)

     On names in above work, passim.

1325 Withycombe, Elizabeth G.
     <u>The Oxford Dictionary of English Christian</u>
     <u>Names</u>. New York, Oxford, 1945.

     See also 3rd revised edition: Clarendon Press,
     1977.

1326 Witkowski, Teodolius
     <u>Grundbegriffe der Namenkunde</u>. Berlin, Akademie
     Verlag, 1964. (Deutsche Akademie der Wissen-
     schaften zu Berlin, Vorträge und Schriften,
     Heft 91)

     A dictionary of name terminology.

1327 Wolf, Norbert Richard
     "Die Gestalt Klingsors in der deutschen
     Literatur des Mittelalters," <u>Südostdeutsche</u>
     <u>Semesterblätter</u>, 19 (1967), 1-19.

     On the name "Klingsor" in German literature
     of the Middle Ages.

1328 Wolf, V.
     "A Review of J. Škutil's 'Miṣtni ...',"
     <u>Zpravodaj Mistopisné Komise Československé</u>
     <u>Akademie Věd</u>, 11 (1970), 806-7.

     On names by Mrštik.

     ---, See: 1098.

1329 Wood, Richard E.
     "Noms de Plume of Esperanto Authors," <u>Liter-</u>
     <u>ary Onomastics Studies</u>, 4 (1977), 105-114.

1330 Woolf, Henry B.
     "Name of Beowulf," <u>English Studies</u>, 72 (1937),
     7-9.

1331 ---, <u>The Old Germanic Principles of Name Giving</u>.
Johns Hopkins University, 1936.

A dissertation.

1332 ---, "Pesonal Names in 'The Battle of Maldon',"
<u>Modern Language Notes</u>, 53 (1938), 109-12.

On names in the above Anglo-Saxon poem.

1333 Worthington, M. G.
"Odiene and Porpaillart: Epic Names in a
Twelfth-Century Chronicle," <u>Romanic Philology</u>,
24 (1970), 101-7.

On names in the Chronicle of Roger of Hoveden
and Guillaume d'Orange.

1334 Wutz, Franz Xaver
<u>Onomastica sacre</u>. Untersuchungen zum Liber
interpretationis nominus hebraicorum des hl.
Hieronymus. 2 vols. Leipzig, Heinrichs,
1914-5. (Texte und Untersuchungen zur
Geschichte der altchristlichen Literatur,
Reihe 3, Bd. 11)

On names in the work of St. Hieronymus.

1335 Yonge, Charlotte Mary
     History of Christian Names. New ed. rev.
     London, Macmillan, 1884. Reprint: Detroit,
     Gale 1966.

1336 Zabeeh, Farhang
     What Is in a Name? An Inquiry into the Seman-
     tics and Pragmatics of Proper Names. The Hague,
     Nijhoff, 1968.

1337 Zachrisson, R. E.
     "Scandinavian or Anglo-Saxon Names? Review of
     Björkman's Writings on Names," Modern Language
     Review, 14 (1919), 391-7.

1338 Zacordonet, A.
     "Numele proprii in opera lui Cehov," Studii
     si cercetari stiintifice filologie, 11 (1960),
     31-43.

     On proper names in Chekhov's works.

1339 Zareba, Alfred
     "Polskie imiona ludowe," Onomastica (Wroclaw),
     9 (1959), 373-408.

     On names in Polish folklore.

     Zeben Buehne, Sheena
          See: 287.

1340 Zemzare, D.
     "Par personu vardiem J. Raina luga 'Pūt,
     vējini'," Karogs (Riga), 8 (1969), 149-50.

     On personal names in the drama of Jānis Rainis.

1341 Zender, Matthias
     Räume und Schichten mittelalterlicher Heiligen-
     verehrung in ihrer Bedeutung für die Volkskunde.
     Die Heiligen des mittleren Masslandes und der
     Rheinlande in Kultgeschichte und der Kultverbreitung.
     2. erw. Aufl. Köln, Rheinland, 1973.

     See pp. 61-3 on names of saints, passim.

---, See: 132, 761, 823, 1053.

1342 Zibelius, Karola
    Afrikanische Ort- und Völkernamen in hiero-
    glyphischen und hieratischen Texten. Wiesbaden,
    Reichert, 1972.

    Based on thesis, Tübingen, 1969. On African
    names.

1343 Zingerle, Ignaz V.
    "Die Personnamen Tirols in Beziehung auf
    deutsche Sage und Literaturgeschichte,"
    Germania, I (1856), 290-5.

    On German personal names in legendary lore
    and literary history.

1344 Zinin, S. I., and A. G. Stepanova
    "Imena personažej v hudožestvennoj literature
    i fol'klore (Bibliografija)," Antroponimika,
    (1970), 330-55.

    A bibliography on personal names in literature
    and folklore.

1345 Zoder, Rudolf
    Familiennamen in Ostfalen. 2 vols. Hildesheim,
    Olms, 1968.

    On German names in literature, see Vol. 1,
    p. 60.

1346 Zola, Emile
    Doctor Pascal. Tr. by Ernest A. Vizetelly.
    London, Chatto, 1925.

    Zola's interpretation of names in literature,
    see pp. x-xi.

SUBJECT INDEX

Abdiel 390
Abraham 828
Abram 828
Abyssinian name(s) 929
Adler, Wilhelm 1225
Adventure with name(s) 930
African name(s) 1342
Agnon, Samuel Joseph 101
Ahasuerus 118
Alas, Leopoldo 639
Albee, Edward 113
Albertine 887
Albertus Magnus, Saint 1007
Alexis 803
Allegory 127 248 323 536 565 713 1000 1294
Alliteration 324
Allusion 247 248 388 1172 1299
Allusiveness 677 887
Alma 1301
Almudena 176
Ambiguous name(s) 2
Ambo 1320
Ambois, de Bussy 1320
American name(s) 63 64 65 68 74 762 886 1010 1084
    1104 1109 1110 1232
American Negro name(s) 63 869
Amyntas 804 1139
Anachronism 35
Anagrams 3
Ancestral name(s) 254 407
Ancient (classical) name(s) 554 1182
Ancient Egyptian name(s) 357
Anderson, Sherwood 830
Andrews, Joseph 267
Andromaque 795
Angel(s) 1293
Anglo-Saxon name(s) 58 284 304 667 1069 1074 1332 1337
Animal name(s) 192 277 280 314 383 400 533 617 765 836
    839 992 993 1086
Anonymity 571 606
Anonymus 231
Anthology, name(s) in 189
Appellative 240 321 924
Appropriate name(s) 168 397 829 866 975 1012 1065
Apuleius, Lucius 1012
Arabic name(s) 446 800 929 973
Aramaic name(s) 407 929
Arany, János 643
Aranyosrákosi Székely, Sándor 878
Archeology, name(s) in 171 172
Argentinian name(s) 798

Argus 1028
Argyve 1028
Ariachne 783
Aristophanes 499 899
Aristotle 24
Armado, Don Adriano de 972
Arminius 498
Arouet 672
Art, name(s) in 171 172 551 752
Arthurian name(s) 5 325 693 694 851 852 853 854 893
    974 1001 1105 1235 1292
Aryan name(s)
    See: Indo-Germanic name(s)
Aspazija (pseud.)
    See: Plieksane, Elza Rozenberga
Assuan name(s) 407
Astrological name(s) 248
Asturias, Miguel Angel 711
Attributive name(s) 413
Aue, Hartmann von
    See: Hartmann von Aue
Aurora Raby 29
Austen, Jane 186 858
Australian name(s) 1014
Authorship 571
Azazel 202

Cabala 556
Caddy 32
Caedmon 388
Caesar, C. Julius 387 1176
Calderón de la Barca, Pedro 713 914
Camus, Albert 565
Canaanic name(s) 929
Captain Vere 182
Carlyle, Thomas 338 1206
Castrén, Matthias Alexander 9
Cather, Willa Sibert 94 353
Celan, Paul 760
Celtic name(s) 51 387 1136
Celtis, Konrad 761
Cervantes Saavendra, Miguel de 2 3 535 644 734 1219
Chanson de Roland 8 705 764 1129 1130 1238
Chanson(s) de geste 151 152 326 654 821 1308
Chapman, George 81 1320
Character(s) name(s) of 41 43 44 307 330 355 398 413
        443 527 546 590 670 712 782 800 801 850 856 857
        889 892 907 959 1062 1156 1159 1249 1263 1271 1315
        See also: Shakespeare, William (characters)
Charactonym(s) 69 382 442 711 1114 1192
Charlatan(s) 1193
Chaucer, Geoffrey 195 207 217 247 248 282 491 514 518
        645 723 736 776 817 894 959 985 1028 1142 1147 1279
Chauchat 76
Chekhov, Anton Pavlovich 619 890 891 1338
Child(ren) name(s) 407 661 886
Chinese name(s) 754
Chivalry(ic) name(s) 239 734
Choice of name(s) 735
Chrétien de Troyes 315 853
Christian name(s) 27 127 311 548 820 886 1275 1325 1335
        See also: First name(s)
                   Name(s)
                   Personal name(s)
Chronicle, name(s) in 571 667 1261 1333
Church play(s), name(s) in 419 1194
Churm 580
Cicero, Marcus Tullius 36 375 871
Cifar 166
Claggart 827
Class of name(s) 937
Classical name(s) 949 1267 1279
Claudel, Paul 1270
Clemens, Samuel Langhorne 206 303 351 784 1115
Cognomina 812
Coinage of name(s) 135 163 257 570 1180
Comedy(ies), name(s) in 205 269 586 590 712 802 1150
        1249

Comic
See: Humor
Common name(s) 167 777
Comolet 81
Compound name(s) 744 1167
Comte 44
Concept of name(s) 304
Concordance 446 473
Conrad, Joseph 1268 1301
Contraversial name(s) 359
Cooper, James Fenimore 203
Corinna 951
Corneille, Pierre 451
Cornish name(s) 893
Correctness of name(s) 20
Corythus 513
Costin, Miron 566
Courtly novel(s), name(s) in 880 1057
Coward 1015
Cowboy 404
Crane, Stephen 1015
Creative process 396 779
Cressida 783
Critical approach 18
Croatian name(s) 12 971
Cromwell 356
Cryptonym(s) 571
Cue name(s) 416
Cue, Nicolaus
See: Nicolaus Cusanus
Cummings, Edward Estlin 45
Curious name(s) 520
Cyclopedia 72 171 172 435 838
Czech name(s) 505 506 625 626 729 1098 1102 1261

Early Christian name(s) 561
Early East Anglican name(s) 1073
Early Germanic name(s) 897
East Icelandic name(s) 275
Eckhart 1128
Edda 668· 923
Edda Elder 923 1177
Edda Minora 923
Eglantine 645
Eglitis, Anslavs 362
Egyptian name(s) 884 929
Elene 487 1296
Elephantine 1092
Ellison, Ralph 1099
Endymion 411
Engels, Friedrich 318 1120
English name(s) 58 60 61 62 254 296 448 614 699 700
    746 968 999 1108 1123 1218 1325
Epic(s), name(s) in 30 31 78 562 579 728 837 880 1019
    1149 1243 1333
Epithet(s) 587
Eponym(s) 1008
Epos, name(s) in 562 646 878 1019
Erex Saga 121 426 943
Ermengarde 919
Escanes 540
Esperanto name(s) 1329
Essays on name(s) 33 306 319 359 510 511 775 823 1045
    1145 1175
Esther 37
Esthetic function of name(s) 420
Ethnic name(s) 139 383 724 876 877 1303
Ethnology of name(s) 171 172 289
Etruscan name(s) 368 494 1160
Etymology of name(s) 27 31 49 78 105 149 166 171 199
    229 235 262 274 293 296 400 448 503 605 626 627
    721 773 1028 1058 1088 1121 1177 1178
Eunedubelianus 231
Eve 16
Evolution of name(s) 254

Fable(s), name(s) in 156 591
Fabrication of name(s) 35
Fairy tale(s), name(s) in 349 363 364
Faliscan name(s) 494
Falstaff 1312
Family name(s) 27 49 50 58 63 97 149 162 188 235 236
 401 464 599 633 692 700 708 925 936 1109 1153
 1217 1345
 See also: Name(s)
      Personal name(s)
      Proper name(s)
      Surname(s)
Famous name(s) 150 551
Faulkner, William 32 43 99 162 412 442 516 889 1208
Faust 311 1200
Fedallah 532
Fiction(s), name(s) in 144 150 171 172 197 198 220 255
 539 545 551 740 866 917 1017 1114 1207 1253 1254
 1262 1263 1297 1298 1306
Fictitious name(s) 1213
Fictive name(s) 698 730 1115
Fielding, Henry 69 185 261 709 1086 1271 1272
Figurative name(s) 244
First name(s) 26 50 52 79 83 97 104 237 260 264 461
 477 576 633 652 882 924 981 1047 1258 1307
 See also: Christian name(s)
      Name(s)
Fitzgerald, Francis Scott K. 11 642 1191
Flacks 28
Flaubert, Gustave 922
Flemish name(s) 239
Fletcher, John Gould 786 901
Flicks 28
Flux 28
Folklore, name(s) in 506 597 626 661 729 741 845 1043
 1102 1202 1233 1339 1344
Folksong(s), name(s) in 12 649 845 1290
Fontane, Theodor 88 243 244 1199
Ford 228
Forename(s)
 See: Christian name(s)
    First name(s)
    Name(s)
Forester, Cecil Scott 330
Forgetting of name(s) 347
Form of name(s) 365 573
Fortinbras 154
Franklin, Benjamin 1251
French Arthurian name(s) 325
French name(s) 102 170 188 235 236 325 1016 1292 1333
Frenkofer 209

Grey, Zane 404
Grimhild
    See: Kriemhilt
Grobis 1236
Groenlendiga Thattr Saga 943
Gromylyoun 1314
Gros Bis 1236
Grumbach, Doris 545
Grzeszczuk, S. 702
Gudrun 47 996
Guide to name(s) 295
Guillaume d'Orange 70 1333
Guthorm 47

Hadubrand 428 1255
Hagen 500 627 996 1121 1122
Hamlet 96 154 462 1218
Hämmerlein 1193
Handbook(s) 150 754 1213 1299
Hangmen 1193
Hankyn 138
Harapha 391
Hardy, Thomas 84 135 158 843
Harmonious name(s) 524
Harpagon 293
Harrington, James 681
Hartmann von Aue 1149 1264
Harvey 1064
Hatzenport 1321
Haukyn 138
Hauteroche, Noël le Breton 269
Hawthorne, Nathaniel 144 921 1114
Hebbel, Friedrich 496
Hebrew name(s) 408 929 1094 1155
Heliand 105 454
Helmbrecht 1295
Hemingway, Ernest 225
Hengest 1226
Henry IV 1064 1312
Hero 124 268 616 1004 1015 1263
Heroic literature (Germanic) 47 116 383 417 458 500
        558 593 634 636 637 638 809 876 877 908 996 1029
        1039 1046 1053 1118 1121 1122 1131 1205 1343
Heroine 1263
Hesse, Hermann 134 779
Hetel 996
Hieronymus, Saint 1334
Hildebrand 428 618 1056 1255
Hispano-Gothic name(s) 905
Historical accuracy of name(s) 1052
Historical fiction, name(s) in 1067
History, name(s) in 171 172 551 752 754 1182
History of name(s) 48 89 104 143 274 296 452 495 599
        692 747 936
Hita, Archpriest of 489
Hoffmann, Ernst Theodor Amadeus 128 755
Hofmannsthal, Hugo von 385 1210
Hölderlin, Friedrich 115
Homerus 153 160 394 406 587 695 696 718 721 799 808
        1063 1125 1317
Homonym(s) 781
Horace
        See: Horatius Flaccus Quintus
Horand 996
Horatius Flaccus Quintus 552 683

Horsa 86 1226
Horses 617 836
Horst 86 836
Howard, Honoria 1062
Hughes, Langston 220
Hugo, Victor Marie 35 73 356 950
Hülshoff, Annette von Droste
    See: Droste-Hülshoff, Annette von
Humor 4 205 413 573 734 738 890 899 917 1207 1286
Hungarian name(s) 231 571 622 643 697 738 1184 1185
    1221
Hun-Germanic name(s) 1039
Hymn, name(s) in 388
Hyphenated name(s) 825
Hysteria 1207

Kafka, Franz 40 93 287 314 409 416 466 541 641 647
    670 833 912 945 947 1282
Kassel 284
Kastrén, Matthias Alexander
    See: Castrén, Matthias Alexander
Kaukasian name(s) 646
Kearney, Kathleen 927
Keats, John 411
Keller, Gottfried 371
Kerkuk tablets 424
Kieffer, Guidino 798
Kipling, Rudyard 595
Klage 637
Kleist, Heinrich 836
Klinger, Friedrich Maximilian von 836
Klingsor 1327
Klopstock, Friedrich Gottlieb 86 836
Knowledge 691
Korolenko, Vladimir Galaktionovich 300
Kostica, Laco 265
Krasicki, Ignacy 367
Kriemhilt 47 85 191 458 463 1041
Krkonoš 505
Krleža, Miroslav 1248
Kudrun 1324
Kumarbi 30
Kyot 615

Macaulay, Thomas Babington 157
McCarthy, Mary 545
Macedonian name(s) 1125
Magic of name(s) 196 280 369 898 993
Majakovskij, Vladimir 1186
Malaparte, Curzio 270
Mallarmé, Stephane 204
Malory, Thomas 693 1315
Manesse 634
Manfred, Frederick 735
Mann, Thomas 40 76 111 478 578 596 628 684 690 750 751
       873 900 980 1002 1011 1141 1227
Manuscript(s), name(s) in 284 329 1093
Marcel 887
Marlowe, Christopher 317 689 1280
Marolf 1205
Maróthy-Šoltésová, Elena
       See: Šoltésová, Elena Maróthy
Martovych, Les' 421
Marx, Karl 1120
Masoch, Sacher Leopold
       See: Sacher-Masoch, Leopold
Matilda 915
Meaning of name(s) 31 58 131 148 342 401 477 519 549
       601 651 652 740 910 978 1123 1217 1257
Medieval literature, name(s) in 438 571 806 998 1165
Medieval name(s) 25 229 233 254 316 326 438 449 454
       605 611 617 669 725 806 865 976 998 1291 1327
Melville, Herman 182 200 211 532 686 827 1000
Menander of Athens 1229
Mendoza, Juan Ruiz de Alarcón y 913
Meredith, George 241
Mesopotamian name(s) 727
Metaphor 982
Metaphorical language 713
Metrical treatment of name(s) 245
Mickiewicz, Adam 399
Middle English name(s) 5 124 138 183 486 820 1074 1134
Middle European name(s) 33 510 511
Middle French name(s) 1021
Middle High German name(s) 133 345 579 638 814 1118
Middle Latin name(s) 606
Middleton, Thomas 673 674 675 928
Mignon 650
Milphidippa 550
Milphio 550
Milton, John 16 202 390 391 524 680 1085 1293
Mitanni name(s) 424
Modern name(s) 18 832 886 936
Molière, Jean-Baptiste Poquelin 146 781 792
Molina, Tirso de (pseud.)
       See: Téllez, Gabriel

Name calling 1078
Name clue(s) 1172
Name giving 324 832 965 1148 1331
Name(s) 38 72 169 321 334 344 361 366 435 450 479 557
    585 607 633 685 691 704 707 760 780 831 838 883
    885 911 929 937 953 961 962 964 982 1058 1113
    1256 1257 1278
    See also: Christian name(s)
               Family name(s)
               First name(s)
               Personal name(s)
               Proper name(s)
               Surname(s)
               Toponym(a)
Naming 201 238 255 273 415 512 546 589 593 661 788 927
    970 1058 1223 1271 1304 1306 1315
Necessity of name(s) 1058
Negruzzi, Constantin 223
Neidhart 1050
Nekrasov, Nikolai Alekseevich 846 848 849
Nektanebos 1285
Nell 181
Němcová, Božena 729
Németh, László 1185
Nennius 854
Netherlands 984 1319
Nibelungen 128 147 301 425 427 463 497 498 522 593
    624 627 636 724 749 810 881 909 969 996 1131
    1274 1287
Nickname(s) 37 126 341 361 586 657 872 963 1073 1084
    1140
Nicolaus Cusanus 504
Niebuhr, Berthold Georg 157
Nietzsche, Friedrich Wilhelm 758
Ninnius 552
Nobility, name(s) of 633
Nomen appellativum 240
Nomen proprium 240
Nomina 812
Nomina sacra 875
No-name(s) 855
Nonce-name(s) 586
Non-Semitic name(s) 929
Nonsense name(s) 1117
Norman name(s) 58
Northanger Abbey 186
North Semitic name(s) 175
North, Thomas 540
Noun(s) 271 937
Novel(s), name(s) in 83 136 203 257 259 542 543 583 598
    603 632 658 798 874 896 970 1014 1191 1286
Number(s) 831

Palestine name(s) 990
Palmyrene name(s) 440 1138
Pantagruel 293
Panurge 293
Papyri, name(s) in 329 407 499 875 884 929
Parallelism of name(s) 161
Paranomasia 340
Parody 539
Parzival 77 335 600 615 648 960 997 1024
Pasithée 1237
Passion play(s), name(s) in 98
Patience 183
Patronym(s) 847 1063 1209
Paul Jean (pseud.)
    See: Richter, Johann Paul Friedrich
Pearl 183 1314
Peculiarities of name(s) 1047
Pequot 467
Percy, Walker 255
Peréz Galdós, Benito 176 874
Pericles 540
Persephone 951
Persepolis 756 757
Persian name(s) 929
Personal name(s) 1 7 10 13 21 22 25 54 60 92 108 133
        134 151 170 188 199 208 212 235 236 246 248 254
        278 282 296 308 316 320 328 331 333 345 395 402
        405 420 421 432 448 455 460 480 481 503 509 528
        534 562 579 594 597 601 631 632 638 651 657 659
        663 664 669 679 692 715 722 746 778 806 845 849
        863 879 880 884 923 925 976 997 1018 1026 1027
        1031 1032 1034 1037 1042 1074 1090 1092 1098 1107
        1108 1111 1124 1135 1138 1166 1183 1186 1187 1218
        1244 1247 1248 1284 1288 1290 1302 1311 1319 1332
        1340 1343 1344
    See also: Christian name(s)
               Family name(s)
               Name(s)
               Proper name(s)
               Surname(s)
Pessoa, Fernando 986
Peterburg 620
Petöfi, Sándor 1221
Petrograd 620
Petronius Arbiter 397
Philosophy, name (s) in 752
Philothée 1237
Phonology 737
Phrase finder 982
Physiognomy of name (s) 110 129 280 281 631
Phyteus 317

Piers Plowman 138
Place name(s)
    See: Toponym(a)
Planet(s), name(s) of 648 1024
Plant(s), name(s) of 262
Plato 20 352 860 903 979
Plautine 550
Plautus, Titus Maccius 739 763 1065 1066 1068 1229
Play(s), name(s) in 221 364 678 913 942 1220
Play with name(s) 710 763 770
Plieksane, Elza Rozenberga 364
Plieksans, Janis 364 455 456 1340
Plinius Secundus, C. 544
Pliny the Elder
    See: Plinius Secundus C.
Plot(s), name(s) in 150
Plutarch 540
Poe, Edgar Allan 360 439 915 916 917 918 919 920
Poem(s), name(s) in 45 78 150 178 183 233 567 568 574
    864 868 923 973 1000 1189 1263 1314 1332
Poetry, name(s) in 138 184 208 230 313 378 551 567 568
    733 807 820 931 978 986 1006 1303
Polexandre 17
Polish name(s) 603 649 702 1339
Political name(s) 962
Pollyana 1091
Polonius 154
Polyanthus 1091
Polyphemus 153
Pomponius Mela 544
Popular name(s) 1112 1173
Porpaillart 70 1333
Porsena 157
Poruks, Janis 272
Posidonius of Apamea 1176
Post Homeric name(s) 1133
Praenomina, Roman 187
Pre Islamic Arabian name(s) 446
Pre Latin name(s) 879
Prise d'Orange 575
Procopius of Caesarea 109
Prolegomenon 1253
Proper name(s) 14 57 77 87 89 106 131 156 161 167 173
    178 184 190 193 217 218 223 226 230 245 247 248
    288 310 325 339 347 350 358 359 365 374 408 451
    521 524 531 549 564 623 625 630 662 739 762 774
    777 831 835 848 885 926 931 938 939 1001 1003
    1014 1016 1019 1051 1076 1077 1096 1097 1105 1123
    1159 1178 1202 1214 1224 1229 1231 1292 1316 1336
    1338
    See also: Family name(s)
               First name(s)
               Name(s)
               Surname(s)

Rabelais, François 355
Racine, Jean Baptiste 788 795 870
Ragnel 486
Raguel 486
Rainis, Janis (pseud.)
  See: Plieksans, Janis
Raminagrobis 293 1236
Reaction to name(s) 863
Real name(s) 228 355
Rebreanu, Liviu 259
Reference(s), name(s) in 140 150
Register 1054
Reinaert 459 591 765
Reinhard 192
Religion, name(s) in 752 867
Reynard 469
Rhetoric of name(s) 795
Rhodope 496
Richard II 1283
Richardson, Samuel 185 261 1271 1272
Richter, Johan Paul Friedrich 95
Riddle(s) 693
River(s), name(s) of 174 191
Robinson, Edwin Arlington 190
Roche, Regina Maria 858
Rodomont 1304
Rogar 348
Roland 465 1238 1241
Romance name(s) 737 769 777 965 1106
Romance of name(s) 1276
Romance(s), name(s) in 325 333 345 694 1263 1292
Roman name(s) 159 187 252 253 590 766 1025 1067 1127
  1135 1181 1182
Romanski, Andrew C. 136
Romanticists 312
Romeo 1281
Root word(s) 79
Rosenkavalier 385
Roth, Phillip 604
Rothari 348
Rothere 348
Royal name(s) 733
Rufus 98
Ruiz de Alarcón y Mendoza, Juan
  See: Mendoza, Juan Ruiz de Alarcón y
Rulfo, Juan 396
Rumanian name(s) 405
Russian name(s) 78 173 205 230 251 292 403 861 892 966
  1018 1019 1096 1230 1243 1244

Sabio, Alfonso el 262 839
Sacher-Masoch, Leopold Ritter von 647
Sacral name(s) 572
Sadoveanu 534
Safarik 505
Saga(s), name(s) in 120 121 276 426 502 547 876 877
     943 944 1321 1323
Saint(s), name(s) of 609 688 1089 1341
Saki
    See: Munro, Hector Hugh
Salarino 55
Salario 55
Salerio 55
Samsa 647
Samson Agonistes 391
Sanskrit name(s) 112
Sargon 509
Sartoris 162
Satire, name(s) in 173 323 573 1135
Satirical name(s) 592 738
Scandinavian name(s) 58 667 1302 1337
Science fiction, name(s) in 640 666 907 1252
Science of name(s) 51
Scottish name(s) 844 968
Scott, Walter 527
Scriptural name(s) 140 340
    See also: Biblical name(s)
                  Testament, New
                  Testament, Old
Seifensieder Unschlitt 76
Selecting of name(s) 621
Self-naming 606 1165
Selloi 1317
Semantics 148 685 725 1336
Semasiology 400
Semitic name(s) 30 929
Sentence name(s) 249 430 1033
Serbian name(s) 971
Serbo-Croatian name(s) 1245
Servius, Grammarian 226
Shakespeare, William (characters) 23 55 96 154 180 199
    234 290 322 413 418 462 485 530 531 540 586 587
    612 613 662 665 671 676 712 716 726 732 753 783
    815 819 828 829 1022 1064 1073 1079 1095 1159 1168
    1179 1218 1245 1281 1283 1300 1312
Shakespeare, William (name of) 6 15 59 82 141 155 164
    165 177 179 214 215 216 222 242 283 285 286 297 298
    346 384 414 431 433 434 436 437 483 507 508 525 526
    529 608 687 719 720 785 805 904 987 1080 1081 1082
    1163 1164 1318 1322
Shaw, George Bernard 1286

Tablet(s), name(s) in 424 471 480 481 482 757
Tacitus, Publius Cornelius 299 1033 1176 1183
Tagore, Rabindranath 862
Tamburlaine 317 689 1280
Tandariáš 1102
Tartuffe 792
Tastes in name(s) 28
Téllez, Gabriel 801 1249
Terence
    See: Terentius Afer Publius
Terentius Afer Publius 34 739 1229
Terminology 305 1326
Testament, New 473 926
Testament, Old 473 759 926
    See also: Biblical name(s)
               Scriptural name(s)
Test(s) of name(s) 278 280
Teufelsdröckh 338
Text(s), name(s) in 594 602 768 1342
Théâtre crétois 630
Theory of name(s) 75 89 131 218 359 374 386 822 831
    938 939 1051
Theresa, Saint 1174
Theriophoric name(s) 813
Thidreks Saga 502 547 876 877 1321 1323
Thing(s) 196 334 352 657 780
Thopas 207
Thracian name(s) 108
Tides in name(s) 28
Timurid 1093
Tirolian name(s) 316
Tirso de Molina (pseud.)
    See: Téllez, Gabriel
Title(s) 142 539 585 633 916 1124 1168
Titurel 77
Tolkien, John Ronald Renel 289
Tolstoi (spelling of the name) 103
Toponym(a) 9 51 123 139 140 174 191 208 275 294 327 337
    410 417 459 506 518 523 538 574 587 593 620 657
    705 714 724 745 748 752 768 807 840 841 842 843
    844 868 876 877 881 902 925 948 949 967 968 974
    990 997 1026 1071 1098 1100 1125 1184 1189 1203
    1211 1219 1233 1287 1303 1342
Translation of name(s) 142 1245
Treasury of name(s) 1288
Tristan 596 1020 1026 1205
Troilus 783
Trollope, Anthony 842
Troubadour(s) 178 1303
Trumpyngtoun 514
Truth 910

Tuka, Abdulah 19
Tunna 1261
Turkic name(s) 139
Turkmenian name(s) 807
Twain, Mark (pseud.)
    See: Clemens, Samuel Langhorne
Typology 867 1059

Valentin 44
Van Doen, Carl 1240
Varied name(s) 324 825
Vašek, Vladimir 625
Vega Carpio, Lope 46 53 307 535 797 800 802 955 1265
    1266
Vergilius Maro, Publius 137 168 447 513 791 1143 1222
Verse, name(s) in 159 325 340 766 1001 1025 1182 1292
Vides de Sants Rosselloneses 835
Vinius 552
Virgil
    See: Vergilius Maro, Publius
Volpone 122
Voltaire, François Marie Arouet de 672 773 1250 1273
von Goethe, Johann Wolfgang
    See: Goethe, Johann Wolfgang von
von Klinger, Friedrich Maximilian
    See: Klinger, Friedrich Maximilian von
von Weissenburg, Otfried
    See: Weissenburg, Otfried von

Wace 1023
Wate 996
Weissenburg, Otfried von 476
Wellerism 1202
Weller, Sam 1162
Welsh name(s) 61 333 974
Welty, Eudora 238 515 555 1253
West Semitic name(s) 212
Wharton, Edith Newbold (Jones) 197
Whitman, Walt 201 501
Wieland 558 995 1044 1046
Wieland, Christoph Martin 836
Wilhelm, Tommy 1225
Williams, Tennessee 221
Wisdom 309
Wit 309
    See also: Humor
Witches 364
Wittenweiler, Heinrich 132
Wittenwiller, Heinrich
    See: Wittenweiler, Henrich
Wolfe, Thomas 954
Wolfram 77 660 834 960 997 998 1024
Word origin 1087
Word play 726 914
Word(s) 366 450 760 885 902 911 918 982 1177 1278
Wormser 1216
Wulfila 376